Pilgrim Voices

Pilgrim Voices

Narrative and Authorship
in Christian Pilgrimage

Edited by
Simon Coleman and John Elsner

Berghahn Books
New York • Oxford

First published in 2002 by Berghahn Books
Special Issue, *Journeys* (Volume 3, No. 1)

Paperback edition published in 2003
by **Berghahn Books**
www.berghahnbooks.com

Library of Congress Cataloging-in-Publication Data
Pilgrim voices : narrative and authorship in Christian pilgrimage / edited by Simon
Coleman and John Elsner.
   p. cm.
   Includes bibliographical references and index.
   ISBN 1-57181-603-8 (pbk. : alk. paper)
      1. Christian pilgrims and pilgrimages--History. 2. Travel writing--
   History. 3. Christian pilgrims and pilgrimages in literature. 4. Travel in
   literature. I. Coleman, Simon. II. Elsner, John.

BV5067 .P55 2002
263'.041--dc21

                                                                    2002027983

British Library Cataloguing in Publication Data
A catalogue record for this book is available from the British Library

Printed in the United States on acid-free paper

ISBN 1-57181-603-8 paperback

Contents

Pilgrim Voices: Authoring Christian Pilgrimage

Simon Coleman
University of Durham

John Elsner
Corpus Christi College, Oxford

And behold, two of them went that same day to a village called Emmaus, which was from Jerusalem about three-score furlongs. And they talked together of all these things which had happened. And it came to pass, that, while they communed together and reasoned, Jesus himself drew near and went with them. But their eyes were holden that they should not know him. And he said unto them, What manner of communications are these that ye have one to another, as ye walk and are sad? And the one of them, whose name was Cleophas, answering said unto him, Art thou only a stranger in Jerusalem, and hast not known the things which are come to pass there in these days? And he said unto them, What things? And they said unto him, Concerning Jesus of Nazareth, which was a prophet mighty in deed and word before God and all the people: and how the chief priests and our rulers delivered him to be condemned to death, and have crucified him. But we trusted that it had been he that should have redeemed Israel: and beside all this, today is the third day since all these things were done. Yea and certain women also of our company made us astonished, which were early at the sepulchre; and when they found not his body, they came, saying, that they had also seen a vision of angels, which said that he was alive. And certain of them which were with us went to the sepulchre, and found it even so as the women had said: but him they saw not. Then he said unto them, O fools, and slow of heart to believe all that the prophets have spoken: Ought not Christ to have suffered these things, and to enter into his glory? And beginning at Moses and all the prophets, he expounded unto them in all the scriptures the things concerning himself. And they drew nigh unto the village, whither they went: and he made as though he would have gone further. But they constrained him, saying, Abide with us: for it is toward evening and the day is far spent. And he went in to tarry with them. And it came to pass, as he sat at meat with them, he took bread and blessed it, and brake, and gave to them. And their eyes were opened, and they knew him: and he vanished out of their sight. And they said one to another, Did not our heart burn within us, while he talked with us by the way, and while he opened to us the scriptures? And they rose us the same hour and returned to Jerusalem.

Luke 24: 13–33 (Authorised Version)

During the Middle Ages, this story became the biblical model for pilgrimage. Christ himself was perceived to be appearing *as* pilgrim, and was frequently depicted fulfilling such a role in artistic representations of the journey to Emmaus. Here we have a truly scriptural model for the alignment of pilgrimage with the telling of tales. The narratives at stake are not only the vivid oral accounts of great events that had just occurred, but also the understanding of those stories in relation to older, established and written accounts, such as the scriptures 'beginning at Moses'. The two disciples on the road to Emmaus, a place about seven miles from Jerusalem, are discussing what is recent history in the narrative of the Gospel but also sacred action from the perspective of a Christian reader – that is, the events of the crucifixion and the discovery of the empty tomb. When they encounter Jesus, he specifically requests a repetition of this narrative, which he then attempts to correct by grounding what is at this stage (in Luke's representation) an immediate and oral sketch, in the deep and literary context of 'all the scriptures'. Only when Jesus blesses and breaks bread – a reference that is both liturgical, in that it is eucharistic, and literary, in that it specifically refers back to the Last Supper in Luke's own narrative (22: 19–20) – do the disciples evince appropriate recognition of their Lord, which is immediately the spur for more discussion and a return journey. After their encounter and identification of its significance, they waste no time in telling others of their experience.

For Helen Moore, in her contribution to this volume, Luke's account has a paradigmatic, originating force: many other pilgrimage accounts have followed, and perhaps borrowed from, a biblical story that links itinerancy with the telling of tales. She also shows how it points to one of the social functions of such narration, since the pilgrim bond is powerfully expressed through the telling of stories within the travelling group. There are still further aspects of the account that are worth reflecting upon here. Note, for instance, the transformations evident in the story: ignorance is replaced by a form of revelation, which is then rendered into a narrative as the men hurry back to Jerusalem to tell their fellow disciples of what has happened. The gossipy, if gloomy, journey to Emmaus becomes an urgent, joyful and sacralised mission to the Holy City. Jesus is the subject of the men's early discussion, the agent of its transformation, and a fellow traveller along the road. He gives proof of his identity – his movement from 'stranger' to known Messiah – not only through a direct encounter with the disciples, but also through locating himself in canonical text: 'And beginning at Moses and all the prophets, he expounded unto them in all the scriptures the things concerning himself.'

These are some of the themes that will recur in modulated form throughout this volume: the interactions between persons, places and texts (cf. Eade and Sallnow 1991, 7–9); the tensions and complementarities between oral and written accounts; the potential for Jesus to be both goal of pilgrimage and exemplary pilgrim; and the ambiguities of journeys, not least given the possibilities of shifts between secular and sacred forms of travel. Above all, we see the self-generating qualities of narrative: the disciples' account of their experience, itself based on Jesus' address to them, becomes both a resonant part of Luke's text and a generator of future accounts and even journeys. As such narratives shift and move into each other, authorship can be shown to be complex and multivocal. The Road to Emmaus (which soon becomes the Road to Jerusalem) is 'coauthored' not only by the disciples, but also by Luke, by those previous accounts (oral and perhaps written) on which Luke's text was itself dependent, and crucially by the revealed and direct utterances of Jesus (his own discussion of scripture) as the risen God.

The 'Road to Emmaus' points to some of the interest that attaches to a study of pilgrimage and narrative within Christianity, while hinting at a more general salience for sacred journeys in other religious faiths.[1] Research on pilgrimage has traditionally fallen across a series of academic disciplines – anthropology, archaeology, art history, geography, history, theology (to list them alphabetically). To date, relatively little work has been explicitly devoted to the issue of pilgrimage as *writing,* and specifically as a form of travel writing. The fundamental aim of the essays gathered here is to move towards redressing this balance in their collective stress on the relation of pilgrimage to the various narratives which it generates and upon which it depends.

The range of narratives that underlies the pilgrimage process is vast. It is, after all, stories that make an event into a miracle and the worker of that miracle into a marvellous figure who can work yet more wonders that will each generate their own stories, as Robert Maniura's paper on the cult of Santa Maria delle Carceri suggests.[2] Such narratives, which may have started orally but subsequently became collected as texts (a kind of textual museum of rarities to go alongside the Church Treasury of relics and precious artefacts),[3] are only one kind of story that pilgrimage generates. They reflect the textual recognition of an apparent immanence of the sacred, which attracts pilgrims to come to a site and perhaps compels the worshipper to bow down to what a sceptic might see as mere 'wood and stone' (to pick up one strand in Charles Lock's piece on the Holy Land). From the individual pilgrim's point of view, there are many other kinds of narratives – other pilgrims' tales of travel alongside one's own tales (the oral accounts, the immediate diary, the careful description rewritten and revised for publication). These narratives reflect the approach to the sacred site as well as framing it. Wes Williams remarks in this volume that 'travelling, listening to others' stories, writing one's own and reading still more are part of one and the same continuum'. Indeed, as both Alexia Petsalis-Diomidis and Williams affirm, a pilgrimage's completion cannot necessarily be separated from the writing of it as a literary replication and renegotiation. That is to say, the world of the spoken and written word is what constructs the ontology of the sacred and its epistemology as something to be approached and grasped. And the images generated at sacred sites – devotional plaques, votive objects, visual records of divine favours received – are often themselves the visual counterpart of oral and textual constructions.

Turning experience into words

When the two disciples rushed back to Jerusalem to tell others of 'what things were done in the way', their act of narration contained little that was premeditated: indeed, they had risen up 'the same hour' and returned to Jerusalem. While such instant description undoubtedly occurs as part of the pilgrimage process – we perhaps see echoes of it in some of the postcards that the Mormons, described by Hildi Mitchell, send home to friends and family – more forethought is usually evident in accounts of journeys, especially when they are written for a public or semi-public community of readers. As the anthropologist Nancy Frey has observed in discussing contemporary pilgrimage to and from Santiago de Compostela (1998: 186), what pilgrims share on return is usually selective and interpretive, and in numerous retellings the pilgrim is likely to edit and elaborate upon the journey's stories. Retelling is thus an important part in the return, allowing one to reinterpret the experiences and simultaneously (ibid.) 'create oneself as pilgrim' (cf. Delaney 1990).

The ideological significance of moulding pilgrimage narratives should not be underestimated, or understood only in the context of individual experience. Riessman (1993: 1–3) refers to the ways in which stories create order by translating knowing into telling, drawing on linguistic and cultural resources in order to persuade the listener/reader of the tale's authenticity while, in the process, fashioning a relationship between teller and audience. Apparently private constructions are therefore likely to mesh with a community of life stories (ibid.: 2). The relationship between narrator and audience may involve a hierarchy that is reinforced or even created through the narrative. Thus, Bowman (1992) argues that, historically, the various images of Jerusalem and the holy places proffered by pilgrimage narratives have communicated the values of powerful élites to wider audiences. In his terms, the structures through which political power was exercised in late classical and medieval periods were linked to the landscapes of the Holy Land in such a way as to lend sacral legitimacy to the apparatus of secular power, while rendering credible and familiar the mythical domain in which Jesus walked and the prophets preached. On the one hand, says Bowman (ibid.: 155), pilgrimage narratives rendered the strangeness of the East familiar to people who knew it solely through scripture; on the other (in an argument perhaps hinting at Victor Turner's [1967: 54] discussion of the orectic power of symbols), they brought the powerful emotions generated by images of sacred places into association with political and ecclesiastical authority structures. As a result, élite pilgrim writers can be seen as writing less about the Holy City than casting Europe itself in the image of Jerusalem. That 'reading-in' to Jerusalem of contemporary issues and attitudes brought from home can be seen in both Petsalis-Diomidis's discussion of the late medieval Felix Fabri and Williams's account of early modern Frenchmen in Palestine, among the essays gathered here.

The power of the pilgrimage narrative, and the perceived need for its control by institutions, can also produce tensions between narrative and experience, as Maniura reveals in this volume. Jacopino, the young boy who in 1484 claims to have seen the image of the Virgin Mary undergo miraculous transformations, finds that he is at first disbelieved – a fate that frequently befalls the often humble visionaries of what will later become established pilgrimage sites (cf. Turner and Turner 1978: 86). The text that Maniura goes on to describe, compiled by the adult and authoritative figure of Guizzelmi, refers not so much to Jacopino but to subsequent miracles, some of which appear to involve Guizzelmi himself, in a narrative appropriation of the salience of the shrine's miraculous powers.

Experience can therefore be turned into words for reasons that transcend the cultivation of individual spirituality; yet, it is equally important to state that words help frame experience. Once the originating theophanic event is recounted, it can direct the subsequent perceptions of pilgrims about a given site, as well as providing much of the motivation for their journeys. Guizzelmi's book is, in part, a listing of what to expect from a Marian shrine that he is both describing and 'advertising'. In her description of contemporary Mormon pilgrimage to sites in the United States, Mitchell argues for the central role of narrative in the making of sacred places, through the deployment of Mormon scripture and myth/history. Sites not only contain branded literature for sale to pilgrims, they are also 'branded' with words themselves, since scriptural texts are actually reproduced as monuments at historical sites. More generally, Mormon pilgrimages, just like those of the earliest recorded Christian pilgrims, such as the fourth-century nun Egeria (Wilkinson 1999), involve the reading of scriptures at significant places, juxtaposing canonical text (often appropriated bodily through reading) and individual experience. If Mormons point to a framing of physical location with text, Charles Lock's discussion of nineteenth-century pilgrimage to the Holy Land presents an equally notable cultivation of a sublime Protestant aesthetic, in which words gain a fetishistic and fertile quality. Lock points to Hazlitt's 'vision of words', a sense of the landscape calling forth text, not as heard but as seen, lettered across the view. In the same way, Victorian Protestant pilgrims to Palestine ideally call forth in inward vision the words of prayers and scripture, removing themselves from the mundane and mediating details of the everyday and the institutional.

There have been times when words have in effect constituted pilgrimage itself. Howard (1980) talks of how sacred travel as an institution was dead in England by the end of the sixteenth century, but lived on in books such as the allegorical and internalised struggle of Christian in Bunyan's *The Pilgrim's Progress.* Similarly (ibid.: 105), Milton describes in *Paradise Lost* the interiorisation of religious experience, with the work ending as Adam and Eve embark on life's pilgrimage. However, the papers in this volume are making a slightly different point, about the ability of narrative (and narrative genres) to constitute experience even while alternative ritual practices are available. The ways in which such experience is cultivated naturally vary according to theological orientation. Maniura's argument is that, in the context of a fifteenth-century European example, pilgrims' accounts can be powerful traces of something beyond the text. Indeed, miracle stories can be seen as the textual equivalents of votive offerings: the telling, like the physical offering at a shrine, acts as a gift, or performance of thanksgiving to the divine. Mitchell's Mormons give testimonies that are personal yet formulaic, reconstituting the convert's life in canonical language (cf. Stromberg 1993); and personal journals about Mormon historical sites reproduce the testimony form, indicating yet another variation on the interplay between person, place and text (cf. Eade and Sallnow 1991). The postcards that Mitchell refers to in her title provide a wonderful image of this juxtaposition and diffusion of narrative: on one side of the card might be a picture of Mormon scripture embodied in a monument; on the other is placed the writing of the individual believer, who perhaps creates their identity as a pilgrim even as they reproduce the significance of Mormon historical sites for their distant reader.

Authors and voices

Text and experience intertwine, then, and authorship may simultaneously be an expression of agency and a form of obeisance to canonical language. The papers in this volume explore closely the ways in which pilgrims can be constituted as authors (and authors as pilgrims), and when pieces are juxtaposed we see some significant historical and theological shifts in modes of narrative production. Wes Williams's examination of forms of belonging in early modern Jerusalem focuses on various travellers who are all attempting to translate the particularities of the place to others, and who all find themselves – in differing degrees – speaking not so much in their own voices as in those of others. Henry de Beauvau is a diplomat rather than a pilgrim, and his description of much of the Holy Sepulchre is decidedly peremptory. In his account, the voices of sacred intermediaries at the shrine are brushed aside in favour of his own perspectives. However, Beauvau is neither insouciant nor truly singular in his attitude: his anxiety revolves in part around his (in-)ability to take on the identity of another kind of traveller to the infidel-controlled Holy Land: not a pilgrim but a crusader – a wielder of a sword rather than a pen. Anthoine Regnaut is a more recognisably Renaissance pilgrim, avoiding the narration of subjective experience and valorising lack of novelty on the grounds that it guarantees membership of a long tradition. The words he produces travel from the Holy Land to France unaltered, so that – akin to a relic – they participate in the power of the sacred location. Regnaut provides yet another example of the ability of narrative to constitute, and not merely describe, pilgrimage experience, and his approach can therefore be juxtaposed with Guizzelmi's miracle accounts and Mormon uses of testimony; at the same time, his absence of authorial intervention – what Williams calls his narrative ascesis

– demonstrates a sense of devotion to, and community with, the reader. Finally, Jean Du Blioul presents two significant figures in his account: there is the first-person voice of the pilgrim, the pilgrim/author who is given narrative space to make mistakes, and alongside him there is the learned mystagogue, the agent of correction towards an exemplary design. Notably, the latter is not a local, but a priest, who displaces with his learning the need for contact with locals.

In highlighting the issue of voice, narrative analysts examine the extent to which the author can claim sole responsibility for a given statement (cf. Bakhtin 1984; Harding 2000: 183). As Tannen notes (1989: 3), current pronouncements can be seen as repeating prior utterances in a variety of ways, including prepatterning, formulaicity and idiomaticity. The original speech or inscription event may be quoted (Keane 1997: 61) or indirect speech deployed. Here, we wish to emphasise two points. First, the ways in which multiple-voicing is a clearly social act, binding authors into a community of words (Tannen 1989: 133) but also, potentially, making audiences and readers coauthors in the sense that messages are shaped to be understandable within particular worlds of discourse. Thus, even in asserting his voice over that of the priest, Williams's Beauvau is still having to locate himself in the context of certain genres of constructing meaning. Second, there is the ambiguity over the authority of the speaker/author in any conscious use of the words of others. Does such an act imply obeisance to, or appropriation of, previous authorities? The answer is often likely to be a mixture of both, but local understandings of agency must be taken into account. Thus, a medieval author who draws on established and formulaic tradition in describing an apparently 'personal' pilgrimage is a discursive and cultural world away from a recent ethnographic account by Susan Harding of contemporary conservative Protestantism. Harding (2000: 12) talks of how preachers appropriate each other's words (and the words of the Bible) wholesale, not least as a means of constructing a spiritually powerful narrative persona that will itself be copied by others (see Coleman, in preparation). The diverse connections between authority and authorship must be examined carefully and comparatively.

What we have said so far reveals some of the alignments that are possible not only between pilgrimages and authors, but also between authors and readers. In addition, contributions to this volume compare authors themselves in relation to varying historical, cultural or ideological circumstances. Williams juxtaposes a number of roughly contemporaneous travellers (and site-mediators) in order to examine the possible modulations of authorship of early modern accounts of Holy Land pilgrimage. Petsalis-Diomidis also brings different pilgrims into her piece, but they are much more widely separated in time, culture and location, since they include Aristides' *The Sacred Tales* (about the process of Graeco-Roman healing pilgrimage), Felix Fabri's famous fifteenth-century narrative of pilgrimage to the Holy Land, and Pierre Loti's account of his personal and initially nonreligious pilgrimage to temples of Angkor, published in 1912. In further contrast to Williams, Petsalis-Diomidis argues that the accounts she analyses each contain within their narratives a developing and changing understanding of the pilgrimage. Travellers' personae as authors and as pilgrims are in a mutually constitutive embrace, although it must again be remembered that the very constructions of personhood will vary widely in cases as widely disparate as these. Aristides' text documents the shift from a concern with one-off bodily healing to a longer-term, revelatory contact with Asklepios. The god becomes a kind of mentor to the aspirant orator, and in this sense the case has parallels with many ethnographic accounts of the translation of healed into healer, distressed person into skilful cult member (cf. Lewis 1971). Fabri also documents a shift from failure to success, but in a very different idiom. A superficial first pilgrimage to the Holy Land — superficial perhaps in actuality but necessarily so narratologically as well – is contrasted with a far more satisfactory second journey to Palestine, and Petsalis-Diomidis notes how Fabri's second pilgrimage relates sights to stories of the Bible, so that viewing and interpreting act as bridges between physical landscape and imaginative landscape, constructed by the Bible and by the pilgrimage narratives Fabri had read. Howard (1980: 40) similarly places Fabri's success in the context of the monk's multilayered narrativisation of his journey: Felix had promised his fellow brothers that he would write a narrative of his travels, and in preparation read everything he could find on the Holy Land. As we have seen, words can prompt experience as much as experience can prompt words. Petsalis-Diomidis's third account, produced by the French naval officer Pierre Loti, is distinctly modern in at least two respects. Whereas Aristides and Fabri journey to the 'centres' of their faiths, Loti is attempting to find some kind of affinity with a foreign belief system, an intention that implies a certain estrangement from his own culture. And this narrative cultivation of a form of self-displacement is reinforced in yet another way: in contrast to the ultimate (if hard-won triumphs) of Aristides and Fabri, Loti can accommodate the possibility of failure in his personal pilgrimage, resulting in a lack of resolution that is passed on to the reader.

Loti's presentation of a journey that does not reach a definitive goal has some parallels with Helen Moore's depiction of Sir Philip Sydney's move from pastoral to epic in his *Arcadia*. Moore notes how a hope for fulfilment in love is replaced by a concentration on process, on the *journey* in search of love. The Renaissance disenchantment that she sees as indicating the birth of the modern is played out within modernity in Loti's acceptance of his lack of fulfilment in matters of spirituality and identity. Moore's account also points forward to another paper, that of Lock, in her emphasis on distance in articulating the object of desire. The Protestantism expressed by Sydney can be shown historically to lead into a number of forms, including that of nineteenth-century traveller-narrators who construct a distanced sublime in which the unreachable becomes transcendent, even as it signals the supposed victory of optical propriety over the temptations of the haptic. In a sense, Loti's failure to find fulfilment is only actuality's mirror of the ideological affirmation of a transcendent sublime never in fact to be achieved but always to be posited, which Lock proposes as the Protestant response to Holy Land pilgrimage.

Petsalis-Diomidis's contribution points to a further concern that is revisited, in various ways, by many of the papers in this volume: the degree to which the personality of the author/pilgrim is permitted to intrude upon the account of the pilgrimage. Williams contrasts Regnaut's narrative ascesis with Beauvau's refusal to lend narrative space to the priest at the Holy Sepulchre. Petsalis-Diomidis notes that classical scholars tend to disparage Aristides because his seeming self-obsession appears more fitting to the twentieth than to the second century, although it is hardly unfamiliar in such repetitive pilgrims as the medieval Margery

Kempe.[4] Guizzelmi, the compiler of tales relating to St Mary of the Prison, presents stories that are deeply entwined with his own experience and family, and he even appears as a character in some of the accounts, but he does not see himself as an author, in the modern sense of crafting a self-revelatory persona that can be consumed by an anonymous and commercially defined public. One of the theoretical problems that Mitchell addresses, the degree to which the individual Mormon can be seen to divert from canonical accounts and experiences, is in part a product of a modern concern with the degree to which there can be a disjunction between individual consciousness and the orthodox role of 'the pilgrim' as ideal type. The 'non-denominational' narrator whom she describes, Troy Williams, uses irony as well as nonstandard narratives to subvert the conventional sacralisation of Mormon sites. In this case, disenchantment results in a (nontriumphalist, ambivalent) assertion of the concerns of the author over canonical forms. There are, of course, other contemporary examples of pilgrimage where either liturgical or narratological divergences from the orthodox are perceived as strengthening, giving new meaning to, an ancient path. Coleman and Elsner (1998) describe how one constituency of pilgrims to Walsingham professes a lack of interest in traditional accounts of the myth/history of the site, but can cultivate powerful experiences through what are perceived to be playful, personalised journeys through its symbolic resources.[5] Similarly, Frey's (1998) characterisation of many present-day travellers to Compostela shows them to be very concerned to engage with 'tradition' in the sense of walking along the route, rather than taking a car or even a bicycle. Yet such medievalising mimesis in a *physical* sense is not necessarily matched in other ways: a modern cultivation of a 'primitive' and 'more authentic' self, possibly divorced from any sense of conventional Christian spirituality, is distinctly removed from a premodern sensibility.

As Howard has argued (1980: 23–5), in a point echoed by some of the contributors to this volume, medieval and earlier Christian pilgrims expressed a worry over the temptations of promoting the authorial and journeying self through warnings against *curiositas,* a form of interest in one's secular surroundings that could lead one away from the path of devotional piety. Fabri, for instance, obsesses over his motivations for travel, and remains unclear whether he is engaged in *evagatorium* (wanderings) or *peregrinatio* (pilgrimage proper). In practice, according to Howard, medieval pilgrimage is highly likely to have been motivated, at least in part, by fascination with travel, and from the eleventh century on many practical guides for travellers and pilgrims appear. Nonetheless, while such guides provide itineraries and name the places to be seen, in most cases little sense of the author's self is provided. Of course, one of the things Howard may be pointing to here is the disjunction between informal oral tales and what a medieval author might have felt was appropriate to commit to paper, but there is nevertheless a significant shift in the role of the author in relation to *curiositas*, as travel becomes divorced from religious institutions and is associated with humanist values of self-education (most famously through the Grand Tour). Curiosity thus becomes a virtue, leading to new forms of exploration of the self and other – and ultimately, along one route, to ethnography. Nevertheless, in our work on contemporary Walsingham, we have found a distant echo of the old disjunction between *curiositas* and piety, not among the 'playful' pilgrims mentioned above but among more self-consciously committed visitors to the site, who engage in touristic activities in the Norfolk countryside but see such activity as 'leisure', to be strictly divorced from pilgrimage liturgy (Coleman and Elsner 1998).

Pilgrimage as travel writing

The narrativised nature of Christian pilgrimage – as something constructed by texts (some canonical and scriptural, some personal and written, many oral and even counter-cultural) – makes it a particular form of travel and of travel-writing. It is almost as if, even by the standards of the modern guide-book culture or of Grand Tour guide-book preparation, Christian pilgrimage has been the supremely overdetermined journey. Travellers may find either what the texts have prepared them to find, or they construct a kind of anti-structure that finds the opposite of the textual range. This opposite is, of course, equally determined by the texts. Thus, pilgrimage is the paradigmatic idiom for the representation of travel in the Western tradition (cf. Coleman, forthcoming), and its failure –

whether cast as disillusion or futility or fragmentation – is the secular reversal of an ideal of sacred fulfilment explicit in the pilgrim's quest (Elsner and Rubiés, 1999: 1–56). The accounts of pilgrims serve both as personal statements of their trips and as additions to the great mass of narrativities within which the making of pilgrimage is generated. The richness of pilgrimage within travelwriting is that it spans the empirical and the fantastical (as it were from Loti or Aristides to Sydney) while constantly playing with a desire for spiritual fulfilment, whose forms of actual achievement may be as mutually exclusive as the 'bowing down to wood and stone' of Lock's Orthodox devotees of icons and the Protestant distance of his Anglican tourists. It is something of the messy richness of that narrative undergrowth underlying pilgrimage that we hope this collection will evoke, at any rate within the Christian tradition.

We finish with a pilgrim's story told to one of us,[6] which encapsulates the complexities of authorship, agency and voice that are evident in all narratives, including those associated with sacred travel. The speaker is an elderly Roman Catholic nurse, and a devoted visitor to Walsingham:

> I have a little story to tell. I was on the eye clinic one day, and I was preparing this man for a minor op. I think I was anaesthetising his eyes or something, and all of a sudden he started telling me about his wife [… who …] was a chronic arthritic. And the family were going to take him down to Walsingham … He went and prayed for her, and at the time he was praying for her, she had a cure. This is what he told me. I mean, it was like out of the blue, he said it to me. I hadn't been to Walsingham then, back in 1982. I was in the Catholic Nurses' Guild but I'd never managed to go with them, but I've always remembered that story, and it's only recently that I've realised it was the first pilgrimage in 1982, for the sick.

This is a tale about many things, including the power of different kinds of words. The man who is the original narrator and main protagonist of the story goes to Walsingham and (in combination with the site) appears to be able to prompt a cure in his absent wife. His journey and prayer have performative, healing effects, but he is also the creator of other powerful words: 'out of the blue' he tells his story to a woman who, at the time, had never been to Walsingham, and who has never herself been a witness of any episode of miraculous healing. The nurse has 'always remembered that story', and in passing it on to an anthropologist (authoring it anew) she sends it on another journey, into an academic text that becomes a witness to the abilities of narrative to describe but also reconstitute what it means to be a pilgrim.

Notes

·1 The world religions, by definition, involve interactions between textual and oral accounts, and all involve forms of pilgrimage (cf. Coleman and Elsner 1995). Given the complexities of conceptualising comparative notions of personhood, agency, text and authorship, this volume focuses on Christianity alone.

2 For a tracing of these issues in the case of Ste Foy of Conques, see Ashley and Sheingorn (1999); and in relation to Sta Maria delle Carceri in Prato, see R. Maniura in this volume.

3 On collecting, textuality and self-fashioning, see Swann (2001: 149–200).

4 *The Book of Margery Kempe* dates from around the 1430s, and is often reckoned the first autobiography in English (Howard 1980: 34). Kempe, like the Wife of Bath, was a married woman who left her husband behind and went on all the major medieval pilgrimages. Interestingly, given the politics of identifying agency and authorship in the premodern period, Howard regards her as 'mad'.

5 It is important to note that we are stating that this is the attitude adopted by one constituency of pilgrims to Walsingham – typically middle-class Anglicans – and that other orientations to the site are also clearly discernible. In addition, our pointing out that such pilgrims claim to develop personalised journeys should not be seen as an acceptance of their unbridled agency: as we show, such apparent postmodern creativity draws on established structures and traditions, while notions of personal freedom are themselves ideologies that can be deconstructed.

6 Coleman, interview carried out in summer 2001.

References

Ashley, K. and Sheingorn, P. (1999) *Writing Faith: Text, Sign and History in the Miracles of Ste Foy.* Chicago: Chicago University Press.

Bakhtin, M. (1984) *Problems in Dostoevky's Poetics.* Minneapolis: University of Minnesota Press.

Bowman, G. (1992) 'Pilgrim Narratives of Jerusalem and the Holy Land: A Study in Ideological Distortion', in A. Morinis (ed.) *Sacred Journeys: The Anthropology of Pilgrimage.* London: Greenwood Press, pp. 149–68.

Coleman, S. and Elsner, J. (1995) *Pilgrimage: Past and Present in the World Religions.* Cambridge, MA: Harvard University Press.

—— (1998) 'Performing Pilgrimage: Walsingham and the Ritual Construction of Irony', in F. Hughes-Freeland (ed.) *Ritual, Performance, Media*. London: Routledge, pp. 46–65.

Coleman, S. (forthcoming autumn 2002) 'Do You Believe in Pilgrimage? From Communitas to Contestation and Beyond', *Anthropological Theory* 2, 3.

—— (in preparation) 'The Fame of Morris: Circulating Texts and Spiritual Agencies in the Construction of a Charismatic Protestant "Public"'. Paper originally delivered to 2001 American Ethnological Association conference, McGill University.

Delaney, C. (1990) 'The Hajj: Sacred and Secular', *American Ethnologist* 17, 3: 513–30.

Eade, J. and Sallnow, M. (eds) (1991) *Contesting the Sacred: The Anthropology of Christian Pilgrimage*. London: Routledge.

Elsner, J. and Rubiés, J.-P. (1999) *Voyages and Visions: Towards a Cultural History of Travel*. London: Reaktion Books.

Frey, N. (1998) *Pilgrim Stories: On and Off the Road to Santiago*. Berkeley, CA: University of California Press.

Harding, S. (2000) *The Book of Jerry Falwell: Fundamentalist Language and Politics*. Princeton: Princeton University Press.

Howard, D. (1980) *Writers and Pilgrims: Medieval Pilgrimage Narratives and their Posterity*. Berkeley: University of California Press.

Keane, W. (1997) 'Religious Language', *Annual Review of Anthropology* 26: 47–71.

Lewis, I. (1971) *Ecstatic Religion: A Study of Shamanism and Spirit Possession*. Harmondsworth: Penguin.

Riessman, C. (1993) *Narrative Analysis*. London: Sage.

Stromberg. P. (1993) *Language and Self-Transformation: A Study of the Christian Conversion Narrative*. Cambridge: Cambridge University Press.

Swann, M. (2001) *Curiosities and Texts: The Culture of Collecting in Early Modern England*. Philadelphia, PA: University of Pennsylvania Press.

Tannen, D. (1989) *Talking Voices: Repetition, Dialogue, and Imagery in Conversational Discourse*. Cambridge: Cambridge University Press.

Turner, V. (1967) *The Forest of Symbols: Aspects of Ndembu Ritual*. Ithaca, NY: Cornell University Press.

Turner, V. and Turner, E. (1978) *Image and Pilgrimage in Christian Culture*. New York: Columbia University Press.

Wilkinson, J. (ed.) (1999) *Itinerarium Egeriae: Egeria's Travels*. Warminster: Aris and Phillips.

The Diplomat, the *Trucheman* and the Mystagogue: Forms of Belonging in Early Modern Jerusalem

Wes Williams
New College, Oxford

Prologue

On 1 July 1592, his first morning in Jerusalem, Jean Du Blioul rose early so as not to miss the first of several 'fine sermons' given that day to the visiting pilgrims by the Guardian of the Holy Sepulchre. For the duration of the sermon, Du Blioul's narrative, which he had begun some months earlier on leaving Besançon, takes on the voice of the Guardian; the listening pilgrim surrenders his narrative first person to the priest, a longer-term resident of the place and professional exponent of its significance. The sermon is consequently not so much recollected as preached anew in the text, its message directed at once to the small band of pilgrims gathered in Jerusalem and to the increasingly contentious and divided community of Christian readers back home. At the conclusion of the sermon, Du Blioul's Guardian introduces the fresh company of pilgrims to yet another character, who will become the hero of the narrative as it develops, and the focus of the latter part of this discussion:

> I will give you one of the fathers, my companions, to guide you through the holy places, and to perform for you the office of mystagogue, showing you the particularities of these places, all to the honour of God and the salvation of your souls. (Du Blioul 1602: 41–42)

What follows, in Du Blioul's narrative of his journey, as in my reading here, takes place under the sign of these multiple mediations. The pilgrim introduces the Guardian of the Sepulchre, who then introduces the mystagogue, who will in turn guide the pilgrims around the holy places. I want, here, to bring all three of these figures into dialogue, and to introduce them in turn to two other professionals involved in the business of early modern pilgrimage to Jerusalem: the diplomat and the interpreter, or, as the French texts call him, *trucheman*. What connects these diverse figures are the politics and poetics of mediation. All are, in one form or another, engaged in the project of translating the 'particularities of the place' to others; under the combined pressures of polemic and mediation, all of these travellers – pilgrims, diplomats, guardians of the Sepulchre, mystagogues and interpreters – find themselves, to varying degrees, speaking not so much in their own persons, nor on their own behalf, but at others' behests, and in borrowed voices.

In a sense, all pilgrims speak in such 'borrowed' terms; to be a Christian pilgrim is to follow Paul's example in the letter to the Hebrews, avowing citizenship of 'another country' and adopting a liminal position not just for the length of the journey, but throughout the pilgrimage of life. Having 'no abiding city', the pilgrim strictly 'belongs' neither at home, nor in Jerusalem. But there is also a more specifically narrative sense in which Renaissance pilgrims spoke in borrowed terms; for almost none of the travellers who published accounts of their Jerusalem journeys were writers by profession. Some – such as Du Blioul – did become engaged in polemic, writing guide books and pamphlets in defence of pilgrimage and against its Reformist detractors, but very few had ever committed themselves to paper, let alone print, before; nor did so again. In speaking of pilgrim narrators developing 'a voice', then, or of 'figures' and 'characters' in their texts, we are speaking about temporary, occasional, linguistic shapes and costumes taken on, or experimented with, by people who do not otherwise appear to have been in the habit of writing, let alone narrating their own experience of travel. As we shall see in what follows, the terms in which pilgrims come to do so, and the descriptions they leave behind of the places they visit, are borrowed from, authorised, and thus sanctified, either by their precursors, or by the guides who lead them around the sites and leave them with memories shaped in ways at once orthodox and new.

If we know little about the writers of these narratives, we know still less about their readers, or the uses to which accounts were put, except in so far as they figure as part of another pilgrim's text. If pilgrims address the question of why they have published their accounts, it is to argue that they do so only in response to repeated requests from friends, or patrons, or as part of that same vow which led to the journey being undertaken. This last point is crucial, since the emphasis on mediation, translation and the emergence of new forms of subjectivity in what follows should not so much obscure as clarify the central assertion of early modern pilgrimage writing: that travelling, listening to others' stories, writing one's own, and then reading still more, are part of one and the same collective continuum. Even non-pilgrims, such as diplomats, *truchemans* and mystagogues become allied to the pilgrim cause; all serve, even in their differences, to articulate pilgrim experience.

1. The diplomat

To begin with, the diplomat, and another scene of arrival. On 15 August 1601, three days after his arrival in Jerusalem as part of the train of François Savary de Brèves, the outgoing French ambassador to Constantinople, Henry de Beauvau was taken to see the Holy Sepulchre. As he reports in his *Daily Relation of the Journey to the Levant (Relation journaliere du voyage du Levant)*, first published in Toul in 1608, once inside, and 'having said a couple of prayers in front of the *Holy Sepulchre*', the company moved on to the adjoining chapel 'according to *Pilgrims*' custom [selon la coustume des *Pelerins*]' (p. 162). Beauvau's remarks here are telling, and they mark his difference from those 'Pelerins' whom his text italicises, as though they themselves were one of the ancient and venerable sites the curious traveller should see in the course of his journey, and should note having done so in his journal.

Beauvau, as his title makes clear, is no pilgrim; his text is a daily record (not a pilgrimage account) of a journey to the Levant (not the 'Terre saincte'). Republished, first in 1615 and then again in 1619, with lavish, expensive views of the cities he passed through, and plans of the various holy sites (all of them the work of Garnich, engraver to the King), the *Relation* was a demonstration more of the author's diplomatic connections and his learned curiosity, than of his devotion. A member of one of the ancient houses of Lorraine, Beauvau, in advertising his attachment to Savary de Brèves, was associating himself with one of the most active and ambitious French ambassadors to the Porte. Although he had not fostered the kind of proto-salon that Aramon, the previous incumbent, had maintained in Constantinople (see Paviot 1987; Tinguely 2000), Savary de Brèves had negotiated a treaty between the Sultan and the French king, Henry IV, which had the effect of making travel through Ottoman lands considerably easier for the French (appended to Savary de Brèves 1628). With a rich haul of ancient manuscripts to guard against penury at home (see his 'Catalogue' 1787), the ambassador was now heading back to France, by way of the Holy Land, and Beauvau seems to have accompanied him at least some of the way.

Having entered the Holy Sepulchre, the ambassador's group made its way, then, 'according to *Pilgrims*' custom' from chapel to chapel. Although the French here – 'la coustume des *Pelerins*' – cannot quite mean that the ambassador and his retinue were in costume, it does suggest a degree of stage-managed performance to their ritual. The sense is reinforced by the diplomat's noting that the company watched as the priests leading them 'put on clothing for the procession', before they all set off, candle in hand and one behind the other, around the Church (Beauvau 1608: 162). Beauvau's somewhat peremptory tone and the hurried pace of his description here contrast sharply with that of those early modern pilgrims who write of their time in this place. Anthoine Regnaut, for instance, describes the procession around the Sepulchre in meticulous detail. His account, first published in 1573, some long time after his 1549 journey, alternates between notation in French of just how many steps he moved forward between points in the shrine, and extended Latin transcription of the precise variations on the liturgy specific to each stopping place, each one preceded by 'it is customary to say [on a coustume de dire] what follows' (p. 71).

Other vernacular French pilgrims, from Nicole LeHuen at the end of the fifteenth century to Henri de Castela at the start of the seventeenth, structure their processual descriptions in near-identical terms. Beauvau, with his almost derogatory 'couple of prayers' seems to have set the discursive habits of pilgrims – the 'coustume de dire' which narrates travel as a form of liturgy – behind him. As the ambassador's retinue makes its way forward, Beauvau duly notes the presence of first one, and then the next shrine in his journal: at each place at which the procession stopped, the company were given 'a devout exhortation' (1608: 163). Several pilgrims take pains, and pleasure, in relating these sermons in detail; some, such as Du Blioul, make of the character who delivers them – the mystagogue – the medium through which to speak more directly to their readers. Beauvau does not. Indeed already at the second 'exhortation', he cuts things short: 'this was done for us at each of the places which we shall mention in what follows' (pp. 163–4).

Unlike the pilgrims, then, the diplomat does not lend narrative space, nor does he surrender his voice, to the priest. If the primary actor of the text is often the ambassador himself – 'M. de Brèves' is the subject of many of the main verbs in Beauvau's account of the company's journey – the diplomat himself is the only guide the reader needs, his the only voice the reader need hear. As if to underline his sense of specific election, his difference from priests, pilgrims and even, on rare occasions, from the French diplomatic circus, Beauvau notes that there were times when he noticed things himself, on his own account, and that he did so alone. At the conclusion of the procession around the Sepulchre, he tells us, he returned to visit two of the holy sites for a second time, not as part of the ambassador's group, but on his own. The first of these places suggests some lingering attachment to pilgrims' understanding of the world in the diplomat; the second reveals his greater allegiance, and an alternative sense of belonging and identity, articulated by way of the rhetoric of crusade.

The first of the sites Beauvau revisits is 'the cut in the rock' made at the instant at which Christ died. He reports, on first seeing it, that 'you can tell that [this cut] is very deep, and many believe that it goes right down to the *Centre of the Earth*' (1608: 166). He, or his printer, marks the place typographically in his text, italicising the phrase and capitalising that Centre in which 'many believe'. Yet even as the diplomat notes the details of pilgrims' belief, he traduces it, or translates it into terms that they themselves would be unlikely to recognise. For they do not write of this place as a geological curiosity, some very deep hole which Jules Verne's heroes might one day penetrate. The pilgrim custom, rather, is to place, like some latter-day Thomas, a finger into the body of the rock. One of many who do this, Gabriel Giraudet, shifts, after confessing to the need for confirmation of this kind, into Latin so as to absolve any lingering doubt about the status of this wound in the earth's surface, and writes: '*Hic est medium mundi*' (1575: 39; see also, for a similar account, Hault 1601: f.65r).

Beauvau first notes this hole in the rock during the procession around the Church. At that stage, like his companions, he was too busy to investigate further, and as the group continued round the church, so too the text progressed: 'Further on, and on the same Hill, we saw another Chapel ...'; but he had not finished with that hole in the rock. 'Once the Procession was over,' Beauvau writes, 'I went to visit the whole Church, *plus particulierement*' (1608: 168, emphasis mine) – a telling phrase indicating that this is a visit undertaken both in detail and on his own. Retracing his steps, he walks back to that 'very deep ... cut in the rock':

> I found that from the Holy Sepulchre to the place where our Lord was crucified, there are fifty-six paces. In that place there is the chapel we have described above, under which there lies another chapel, that of Saint John the Evangelist, where you can see the continuation of the cut in the Rock, at which place, people say, the head of our *First Father Adam* was found, and the length of this chapel is forty-two paces, and its width twenty-three. (Ibid.)

An image, then, of a man leaving the company of priests and temporary pilgrims, then pacing, carefully and alone across the Holy Sepulchre, to take another look at something he has noted in passing. Notebook in hand, perhaps – he does not say when he writes things down – he places his measuring self among the verbs of common knowledge: 'you can see ... and people say' run alongside 'I found ... and the length of this chapel is ...'. The diplomat's verbs of personal witness at this stage alternate with, rather than correct, those of pilgrim tradition. Once in this lower chapel, he first notes its precise dimensions and then painstakingly transcribes the Latin inscriptions which can, just, be made out on the stones which form its floor and walls. But why has he made this extra journey to this, the second of the places he notes having visited for a second time on his own? And why take the trouble to note down the writing on these stones?

As the large Latin italics which take up almost half a page in his text make clear, this chapel holds the tombs of Godefroy de Bouillon and Baudoin, whom Beauvau glosses as the 'Champions of the faith, born of the ancient and royal House of Lorraine' (1608: 168–69). The diplomat spends some long time in this chapel, and gives it the kind of attention pilgrims give to holy sites. He takes note of details when he can – the epigraph on a further tomb, that of one of Baudoin's sons, is carefully transcribed – and notes also when he cannot: 'The other one is that of Baudoin's wife, but the writing on it is so spoiled that there is no way to read it' (1608: 170). Having seen 'all these things', Beauvau went back to the priests' chapel to sleep, 'since it is the custom for all Pilgrims, that they should spend at least one night in the church' (ibid.).

Beauvau goes along, then, with pilgrim custom, but, as the measured phrases make clear he is, rather than a – by the early seventeenth century, old-fashioned – Jerusalem pilgrim, something more old-fashioned still. For the tomb he has crossed his world to honour is not that of Christ, but that of his dynastic fathers, the heads of the Crusading House of Lorraine. Part of the ambassador's train, he is not subject to the laws and taxes imposed by the Ottoman authorities on pilgrims; arriving, at the end of part three of his *Relation*, at the gates of the Holy City, he proudly notes that he did not have to pay to enter either the city or, later, the Sepulchre itself: '*Monsieur de Brèves had brought with him an order from the great Lord* [in Constantinople], which exempted us' (1608: 147). These notes are, however, signs of more than one man's pride at his profession and at his powerful travelling companion. The pride of place given in the text to the Lorraine House of Baudoin and his successors indicates more than Beauvau's particular dynastic allegiance, which distinguishes him from the other, French, nobles on the journey. For in his repeated efforts to differentiate himself, both from pilgrims and their ways of seeing, and from the others in his diplomatic group, Beauvau bears quiet, yet insistent, witness to an anxiety, and a desire, which is only otherwise given voice at the edges of his narration, at each end of the description of the Holy City.

The anxiety concerns his privileged profession, and the desire is to have the journey, the progress through the land, prove far more difficult than it does: to be obliged to capture the particularities of the place not with pen and notebook, but by the sword. The gates which close part three of the *Relation* open, as noted above, freely to the travelling diplomats; yet part four, which was to tell of their time in Jerusalem, opens with the author in such distress that he does not want to continue at all, let alone enter the gates of Jerusalem. Rather, Beauvau confesses, 'I enter into so great a melancholy as to almost lose all desire to write' (1608: 151). The cause of his distress is that 'all these places are in the hands of infidels'; if Christian Princes would only leave their differences 'at the gates of the City' and unite to regain the land once again, then:

> How much more willingly would I then take up my sword to follow them in their generous enterprise, than simply take up my pen as I do now to inform you of all the things I have seen. (1608: 152)

To some extent this, like the profession of melancholia which precedes it, is poetic self-defence, proper to a man of Beauvau's nation and station. For alongside the praise of the House of Lorraine there runs the general disdain of writing appropriate to the diplomat's noble caste, and the particular argument concerning the uselessness of narratives of the self. The man knows that if his text is not a prayer to God, or a panegyric to his Prince, he should not be writing all. Much as it is in part his task to commemorate the movements of Ambassador de Brèves (which he does, and does well), so it would be his secretary's role, not his, to note down the details of his days. But Beauvau – unlike, say, that other occasionally melancholic nobleman, Montaigne – travels without a secretary (for more on Montaigne on pilgrimage, see Williams 1999a). Nor indeed is Beauvau alone in detailing the Ambassador's movements: de Brèves's name heads another account of this journey, the *Relation of the Travels of Monsieur de Brèves, in Greece, The Holy Land, and Egypt, as well as in the Kingdoms of Tunis and Algiers ...*, first published in 1628, and then again in 1630, of which he is generally thought to be – and is usually catalogued as – the author. In fact de Brèves never there speaks in his own voice, and it is the self-styled editor of the *Relation* – one du Castel – who seems to have written much of de Brèves's story; but Jacques du Castel carefully maintains his secretarial distance, and, unlike the diplomat, never tells of things he does, sees, notices, or regrets, on his own account, or in his own voice.

Beauvau, by contrast, exploits opportunities of collective action in order to indulge in singular narration; and he does so almost exclusively in his own voice. He writes extensively of his travelling companions' actions, and others from outside the ambassador's retinue do from time to time appear in the account to tell him what he needs to know to be able to tell his readers – for instance, when the information is famously a secret, such as the measurements of the Dome of the Rock (1608: 155). But the truth about the places in Palestine is never articulated by the Christian locals; neither priests, nor the interpreters who work for them are given voice in the text. While it is almost always 'we' who walk through the sites, it is almost only ever 'I' who speaks to the reader. 'One morning,' Beauvau writes, 'we left the Monastery led by two Religious and an Interpreter' (1608: 172), and appears in so doing to make a rare acknowledgement of the fact that his experience of the place of which he writes is mediated by others, and indeed by other professional mediators. But the information which follows (and which we, his readers, might assume they, his guides, gave him) is not, within the narrative, motivated by their presence. The day's site-seeing outside the City gates, on the Mount of Olives and beyond, exhaustively detailed in the account, is prefaced by an address from author to reader: 'It is now time for me to call on you to go further afield, so as to show you all that there is to be seen here in these parts' (ibid.). The verbs of observation which follow are in the first person plural, but the 'we' in question here connotes (first and foremost) Beauvau and his reader.

We might reasonably see this singular style as a further function of his caste and his profession; perhaps, for the diplomat, private, face-to-face, communication is the best guarantee of truth. But this is also a feature of his narrative strategy in that mediated form of speech which is the printed journal, the book. For no one the author meets is ever staged, nor reported speaking; what they say is never transcribed in the text, neither as dialogue nor as 'devout exhortation'. No one speaks to us but the diplomat; we read no one's words, hear no one's voice but his. It is in the context of this degree of narrative singularity that Beauvau's repeatedly declared desire to wield sword rather than pen, and his private journey to the chapel beneath the Rock, can best be understood. Betraying perhaps an anxiety about his formal originality – this is one of very few published accounts of the Jerusalem journey to have as its structuring principle the journal, the observations of one man on the road – Beauvau creates for himself an alternative identity, an alternative character to that of either pilgrim or self-effacing secretary. It is that of the bluff crusader, at once repressed other and fantasy self to the early modern diplomat in his courteous dealings with the Ottoman Empire, who spends a good deal of his narrative arguing that he would really rather not write at all.

2. The *trucheman*

Beauvau's *Relation journaliere* is emblematic by its difference from pilgrims' accounts in its confession of being written out of curiosity. He misspells the term in the preface to his second edition, but 'curisiote' there displaces even service to his Prince as the primary reason for the journey (1615: unpaginated 'Preface'). Emblematic, too, is his argument that one man's story of his own wanderings across various places might be of interest to others. Pilgrims have, on the whole, no such confidence; or rather, they argue strongly against the very grammar and structure of such writing, for it is these that betray the sins of pride and curiosity that infect so many travellers, and risk making of pilgrimage something which is, spiritually speaking, worthless, or worse.

Renaissance pilgrims rarely write about things they have done on their own. The structure of the sentences in which they tell of their experience is scrupulously plural, communitarian, as can be judged from the account of Anthoine Regnaut, whom we saw earlier making his way round the Sepulchre. Like Beauvau, only some fifty years before him, Regnaut had avoided having to pay to enter the Holy Sepulchre. But this was, he tells us, good fortune, not design: he happened to arrive at the same time as the earlier ambassador, Aramon, and so was granted free entry (Regnaut 1573: 67). But he is most definitely a pilgrim, and even as he joins himself to others at the Sepulchre gates, so too he takes care to stress the collective rather than personal value of his experience, appending to his own account an eleven-point guide for prospective Jerusalem pilgrims. The first of his instructions has nothing to do with the practical necessities or dangers of the journey itself, but concerns itself rather with the spiritual costs of curiosity and narrative desire. Pilgrims must, he says, steer clear of the new fashion for first person singular narration from which travellers these days too often suffer. If they do leave home, they should do so, Regnaut argues:

> with the intention of going to see and to visit with great floods of tears those Holy Places which God has elected and chosen in this world for the redemption of human kind, and not with the intention of seeing the world, or so as to exult in saying 'I've been in such and such a place, I've seen this or that thing' and so on, gaining in the process estimation in the world, as some do. For anyone who does so, as our Lord says in the Gospels, *Receperunt mercedem suam* [will have long since received their reward]. (1573: 1)

Rather than display such signs of novel, personal experience in the course of his narrative, the traveller should, he tells his bishop and patron in a prefatory letter, think of being a pilgrim as its own reward. He should revel in ancient ways of speaking and reveal how 'his heart walks in a straight line', how his text is 'neither decorated with fine paintings, nor enriched with sweetly ornamental or affected language' (1573: f.a2r). Above all, then, in telling of 'the truth of things seen', he must avoid the narration of subjective experience.

These are not new arguments, of course. Indeed, as I have argued elsewhere (Williams 2000: 205–10), it is their lack of novelty that assures their value to the pilgrim in so far as he proves to be part of a long and still living tradition. But in redescribing the pilgrim's stylistic poverty as infinitely precious, Regnaut is also, albeit indirectly, arguing the worth of personal witness, of the travel account as *autopsy*; he does so in common with – which is to say also in competition with – Renaissance travellers to the New World, such Jean de Léry in Brazil, who assure their readers that their narratives were composed in the promised land itself, and that they have written of things: 'in the order in which they happened, without embellishing, or adding, or subtracting anything from the journey itself' (Regnaut 1573: f.a2r; see also Léry 1992: 21–34). The text, in other words, has not been tampered with, not even – or perhaps especially not – by an Author. Regnaut's account has made its journey from Palestine to France with the analogous trajectory from manuscript to print unaltered, and so, akin to a relic, it carries with it the charge of the power of the sacred location in whose substance it participates. The programmatic absence of retrospective authorial intervention, a kind of exemplary narrative ascesis, demonstrates the pilgrim's sense of devotion to, and community with, his readers. It also, crucially, leaves room for others to speak of the holy places, both in the places themselves, and in the place of the author.

This matters because a central innovation of the counter-Reform, one which effected a major change in the practice of pilgrimage, was to make of mediation a hallmark of the sacred. The pilgrim, increasingly cast as a traveller in spiritual danger, a simple believer in need of guidance on the journey, would, it was argued, lose his way if he were not assisted by others. These others were not authors, nor yet amateur guides and travel writers, but professionals such as interpreters, priests and mystagogues authorised by the church. They alone were in a position to explain to the pilgrim the true sense of what he might otherwise be in danger of thinking as, and narrating in terms of, his own experience. It is this process I want to look at now, first in relation to priestly readers of Regnaut's account, and then, finally, in relation to the pilgrim figures with whom this brief exploration began, Du Blioul and his mystagogue.

The argument concerning the forms and the terms of personal experience is central to the early modern period. It informs fields as apparently diverse as medicine and prayer, as reading the Bible and shopping for the best deal on the package tour from Venice to Jaffa and back. For the priests of the counter-Reform, who sought to reanimate the practice of the Jerusalem pilgrimage in the first years of the seventeenth century, to rescue it from its detractors, and who, following Regnaut's example, accompanied their own accounts with *Guides* or *Instructions* on how to perform the journey, one thing above all was clear: there was an urgent need to define the subjectivity of what Henri de Castela, the most persuasive of all these pilgrim legislators, termed, 'la personne chrestienne [Christian character]'. It was in the nature of Renaissance argument that the priests understood subjectivity to be a question both of action and of speech: to be a pilgrim was to do certain things, perform certain actions, and to speak – or not speak – in certain ways. The most extreme of the injunctions Castela offers in his *Guide and handbook for those wishing to undertake the Holy*

Pilgrimage to Jerusalem, published separately from, and in cheaper format than, his own account of his 1600 journey, was to suggest that the pilgrim avoid all contact with anyone he might meet on the journey: 'the best thing would be to counterfeit, when amongst others, the deaf, dumb and blind man' (Castela 1604: f.60v). His avowed concern is with the pilgrim's intentions, and, once again, with the danger pilgrims face of turning into travel writers. Early in the text he hardens Regnaut's warning:'God does not inspire us to undertake the Holy Pilgrimage so that we can prattle and boast afterwards about having seen this or that rare or singular thing' (1604: f.4v).

Castela's colleague-in-arms Loys Balourdet, a priest who made the journey in 1588–9, echoes, almost verbatim, Regnaut's advice concerning not speaking in the first person about your experiences. He concludes the preface to his *Guide to the Roads on the Jerusalem Journey* with the now familiar argument that those pilgrims who travel in order to then be able to speak, or write 'in exaltation of saying I have seen this or that thing' have already 'long since received their payment and reward' (1601: f. Eiir). These last words, a quotation from the gospels, are, as noted, near-identical to the advice given by Regnaut; but the differences reveal how quickly the history of subjectivity within a form such as vernacular pilgrimage narrative can move. For where Regnaut cites Christ's words against seeking the reward which comes from acclaim, he also explains that this is what he is doing: 'as our Lord says in the Gospels', he writes, and he leaves, as we saw above, the text in Latin. Regnaut is careful to acknowledge his sources, whereas Balourdet, in silently imitating the earlier pilgrim's account, suppresses not only his earlier pilgrim source, but also the reference to scripture; he then translates Christ's words almost as if they were his own vernacular advice. He might have named his precursors (the earlier pilgrim and Christ himself) as part of his elegy to some lost pilgrim style. Instead, and in order to fortify his own authority, he subsumes their voices to his own, even as he warns his reader against precisely that 'exaltation of saying I' which he, in common with other priests, perceives to be the primary threat to a pilgrim's integrity.

Regnaut, not himself a priest, and writing and travelling before the counter-Reform took hold of pilgrims' intentions and policed their texts, is more willing than later priestly pilgrims both to acknowledge his debts to past pilgrims, and to engage in contact with local Christians and others on the journey. Indeed, his is one of the few early modern Jerusalem pilgrimage accounts to acknowledge the degree of his dependence on, and contact with, local people in Palestine. He gives extended attention, and textual space, to one local character in particular, the *trucheman*, or interpreter (for more on this term, see Gomez-Géraud 1987). The interpreter who accompanied Regnaut and his fellow-pilgrims was clearly part of the Franciscan pilgrim set-up, and assisted them in all their dealings with other locals, alerting them to the multiple meanings of the places they visit. Cited as a source of information – albeit rarely given voice – time and again in the pilgrim's narrative, he was a man who, Regnaut notes, with obvious admiration:

> [knew] how to speak Turkish, Arabic, Greek, Italian and French to speak, and reply for pilgrims when they are being led through the Holy Places in Jerusalem and on the journey to the Jordan and to Hebron. (1573: 50)

So, inevitably, when the travellers come to the centre of the pilgrim world, the Holy Sepulchre itself, they are accompanied by their *trucheman*. Once inside, he leads them not to the Crusader chapel which would attract the diplomat Beauvau's attention, but to one which lies deeper still, a few steep stairs further down into the rock. It is here, people say, that St Helena inaugurated the practice of pilgrimage by discovering the location of the cross, 'which', Regnaut reports, 'Jews had hidden there so that the memory of it would be lost for ever' (1573: 90–91). The air in this chapel is 'wondrous cold' and in the wall of the stairwell that leads back up into the body of the Church there is a hole:

> shaped like a window, in the stone, where you can put your head and in which we put ours, and there you can hear a noise, as if someone were hitting something. Our interpreter gave us to understand that this was the place where the miserable man [Malchus] struck our saviour Jesus Christ during his Passion. (1573: 92)

The original French text, to which I shall return in a moment, here reads as follows:

en façon de fenestre, dans vne pierre, où lon peut mettre sa teste, dans laquelle nous y mimes la nostre, où lon oit vn bruict, comme si lon frappoit sur quelque chose. Nostre trucheman nous donna a entendre qu'illec estoit le lieu, où vn malheureux donna vn soufflet à nostre Seigneur Iesus Christ en sa Passion.

Like Beauvau, then, Regnaut goes deeper into the rock, finds a deeper hole than that which first appears to the pilgrims. But unlike the diplomat, he does so in company, and is led there not by a sense of dynastic history, but by a local guide. The villains of the lower chapel to which he and his companions are led are not the contemporary Christian Princes of Beauvau's *Relation*, whose 'ambitions particulieres' so divide them, and so leave the land 'in the hands of infidels' (1608: 151). Rather, it is the Jews, foiled in their attempt to suppress Christian commemoration of the place; its hero is the interpreter. For it is *his* singular attention to the meanings of even the gaps in the walls that reveals how the blows once dealt to the face of Christ can be heard resonating through the history of these stones.

But the *trucheman* is not, any more than the stories he tells, altogether unproblematic. Indeed, as Gregory of Nyssa had argued in the fourth century, and as Erasmus and other Reformers continued to argue throughout the sixteenth, the meanings attached to places of pilgrimage are founded, more often than not, on rumour, much of it the function of local and political concerns (Williams 1999b: ch. 2–3; see also Maraval 1986; Gomez-Géraud 2000: 167–89). Which is to say that the very aspects of the *trucheman*'s narratives which made them precious to the pilgrim Regnaut – their being both locally generated and site-specific – are what make them suspicious to Reformers. If we read with a Reformer's ear to the possibly unwitting polysemy of the pilgrim's self-avowedly simple text, if we read the French and remember that 'entendre' means both to hear and to understand, and that a 'bruict' is both a noise and a rumour, then a different sense of the interpreter's words, and of his role, emerges. For it is not the gospels, nor even the priests themselves, who tell pilgrims of the treachery of the Jews, and who cause them to 'entendre' such 'bruicts' as that of the hand of the 'miserable man' who did violence to the face of Christ, and whom other pilgrims name as Malchus, resonating in the hole in the wall. Rather, it is the *trucheman*, whose mediatory role allows him to mark his difference from others who live in Jerusalem, to make at least a living, and perhaps a killing, from the business of pilgrimage as he sustains and reinvents the *lieux de mémoire*, the commemorative sites, for the foreign visitors with lingering designs on the land.

Narrative energy, the maintenance of a rhetorical tradition, and the associated, inherited aggression towards others of other faiths are, in Regnaut's text, displaced not on to the figure of the ancient and foreign crusader, but on to the local, living, *trucheman*. With his intercalated narratives and site-specific details – that of the hand of Malchus is just one, located at the Sepulchre's centre – the *trucheman* provides the early modern Christian pilgrim with the rhetorical means to present the Jerusalem journey, not in personal, nor even in national terms, but as a polyglot, international performance in unstated, yet still defiant, defence of the continuing relevance of pilgrim tradition. In the context of early modern pilgrimage this displacement had, as I suggested above, its dangers, for it played into the hands of those Reformers who argued that pilgrimage is, more often than not, politics, and that the devotional energies of believers are all too easily diverted, by professionals with other designs, to temporal and territorial ends. They had – and, as the continuing history of Jerusalem suggests, still have – a point.

3. The mystagogue

Some idiots, once they get home, want to talk about the journey, and will tell you that [Jerusalem] is situated at the middle of the world, because it is written that God brought salvation from the centre of the earth, and they will tell you that in Jerusalem there is a very deep well …

The words are those of the pilgrim with whom we began this journey, Jean Du Blioul (1602: 43–44). Marking his difference from others who return home and tell of their experience, he redefines, with the help of the mystagogue first introduced to him by the guardian of the Sepulchre, that 'centre of the world in which many believe', of which Beauvau wrote. Together, they pour scorn into that 'deep well', the hole in the wall which

Regnaut, thanks to the *trucheman*, had heard resonating with the sound of violence done 'by the Jews' to his Christ. Central to Du Blioul's text, and to his argument concerning the meaning of post-Reformation pilgrimage, is the figure of the mystagogue, a man who is, crucially, not a local, nor simply someone adept at speaking several languages, but a priest, and 'an aged and learned man, who had spent several years in Jerusalem, and wanted to end his days there' (1602: 74). Guided by the mystagogue, led by him through the sites, their orthodox meanings, and the modern means of establishing the coordinates of belief, Du Blioul is able to dispel the first of the 'idiot' claims by calculating, with the help of an astrolabe, that Jerusalem is in fact situated at 32°, 35' latitude and 57°, 25' longitude. Assuming the voice of the mystagogue, the better to further correct his pilgrim precursors' errors, Du Blioul writes: 'as regards that which is written about the middle of the earth, you must understand that Jerusalem is situated as if in the middle of the habitable world' (1602: 45).

This is measurement not in the pilgrim paces of a Regnaut, or even a Beauvau, but calculation according to the rhythms of the new sciences of travel – astronomy and ethnography. Crucially, whereas its results can be accommodated to authorised understandings of scripture, local, popular legends cannot. Du Blioul's discussion of the hole in the rock at the Sepulchre's centre ends with a *boutade* in the voice of the mystagogue: 'of the trembling hand of Malchus there can be no talk in this Holy Land' (1602: 45). The mystagogue thus displaces with his learning the *trucheman*, and with him, all need for contact with, and contamination by, the suspiciously polyglot locals, their unauthorised legends, and their foreign concerns. Pilgrims need never speak to anyone but their own kind, or their professional minders; and the reader needs only to join the pilgrim company and listen to the orthodox explanations of the mystagogue.

But this is not the end of the story; if it were, it would make of pilgrimage a purely liturgical practice and of Du Blioul's narrator a mere mouthpiece for counter-Reformation orthodoxy. In fact, his *Voyage* is more complex: both more anxious about, and more sophisticated in, its narrative and polemic strategy. In particular, the dialogue of correction begun above between Du Blioul and his precursors never quite ends. For it extends beyond the figure of the local interpreter and on to the learned traveller, the 'idiot' come home with his opinions; it then takes in, by further extension still, those critics at home who think that the study of history, as of scripture, is itself sufficient to salvation, and that actual, physical displacement to sacred sites is an irrelevance. Such is the reach of Du Blioul's polemic, but the mystagogue also plays a central role in the internal dynamics of the pilgrim's text. For he reinvests the experience of (reading) pilgrimage with a certain romance, by opening up within it a space for error: people need to get things wrong so that the mystagogue can correct them; the pilgrims need to lose their way, or behave inappropriately, so that he can guide them back to the path of proper conduct. For Du Blioul himself the narrative rewards are remarkable.

Eight years separate the journey and the publication of Du Blioul's account, but rather than writing from the position of knowledge gained by experience, he displaces almost all wisdom gained by experience on to the figure of the mystagogue. This allows him to write of himself as something of a pilgrim *ingénu*, a naive, credulous and over-curious figure who persists in getting things wrong, in misreading the places, and in breaking the rules of pilgrim conduct. The learned mystagogue, meanwhile, always on hand to correct the wayward pilgrim, gives Du Blioul the space to make mistakes, to tell, in his own, first-person voice, of his having done so, to recuperate the error to a corrective, exemplary design, and to report, in the words of the wise old priest, his own absolution.

One scene, of many, will serve to show how this space – the romance trope of error contained – is created within the pilgrim's text, and indeed how Du Blioul makes of misunderstanding a structuring principle of pilgrimage narrative. He and his fellow-travellers are engaged in a paradigmatic pilgrim activity: gathering stones as relics. In Gethsemane, they wonder at the marks left by Christ's elbows, knees and hands in the rock, and make to take some of the stones away as souvenirs. Counter-Reformers, responding to the critiques of relics mounted by Calvin and others, had strongly argued against this practice. If, as Du Blioul points out in the (unpaginated) 'Preface' to his account, 'it is not superstition to want to honour God in particular places', then this must be because of the non-transportable particularities of those places. As relics, these stones bear the mark of Christ's real presence. It is the fact of the enduring presence of the sacred here inscribed that justifies, indeed requires, the kind of attention – political and religious – pilgrims afforded to the stones. This is the theory as developed by theologians, including Du Blioul himself in his own earlier Latin polemic, the *Hierosolymitanae Peregrinationis Hodoeporicon* (1599; for a fine reading of this see Gomez-Géraud 2000: 841–60).

But here, in the place itself, in the vernacular account of his own time spent there, Du Blioul casts himself in the role not of the professional theologian, nor of the learned scholar. Just one of a group of simple pilgrims, he writes: 'we tried with knives and other instruments to break off some little pieces' (1602: 57). This is the cue for the mystagogue, and the voice of correction, to intervene: 'But our mystagogue warned us that we were labouring in vain, and contrary to the will of almighty God, and that this rock, so engraved, would remain whole until the end of the world' (ibid.). In biblical language which echoes that of Christ to his own disciples, the mystagogue explains how the pilgrims' actions show that they have misunderstood both the particularities of this holy place and the theory of pilgrimage, again. The pilgrims' response – including that of the pilgrim Du Blioul – is to listen, to record the moment of correction, and to repeat the error in a different mode: 'So, we scratched at the rocks adjacent to this one, and took away several little pieces in remembrance' (ibid.).

What we now tend to characterise as peculiarly modern forms of subjectivity – narratives of doubt, of anxious rebellion against percursors, or tradition – are formulated in the intricate moves and counter-moves of Reform and Counter-Reformation that trace a pattern of contestation across the long sixteenth century. Pilgrimage figures for some then, as for many now, as the paradigmatic medieval form. And indeed Renaissance pilgrimage narratives at first reading can appear rebarbartive, distinctly lacking in innovation, products of a peculiarly conservative narrative mind-set, out of time with an age of discovery, invention and proto-modernity. Yet it is precisely through the most apparently conservative of forms and figures that change may most effectively be introduced to a culture: few people think to look for signs of lasting change in such places, and fewer still notice the subtle differences at first. Before long, they have become second nature.

There are, attached to the chapels, walls and rocks of Jerusalem, as within the texts of the travellers we have followed here, different readings of the relations between sacredness and place, innovation and tradition, error and correction, the theory and the practice of pilgrimage. Each of these writers feels the force of change, and of memory, in different ways. Each creates for himself a textual companion – be it crusader, *trucheman* or mystagogue – to carry the burden of generic self-consciousness, to deflect the charge of curiosity, indulgence or narrative desire. It is the textual companions, too, who mediate the force of criticism and attack at home and abroad, and so keep a particular understanding of the pilgrim tradition alive, even as pilgrims themselves persist in getting it wrong. The peculiar force of Du Blioul's mystagogue is that it is through the voice of priestly orthodoxy that the terms of science and the new learning are introduced to the discourse of pilgrimage: it is the mystagogue (and not the pilgrim himself, nor the diplomat, nor yet the lay guide) who defines those transformations in subjectivity and in the understanding of pilgrim tradition which the Counter-Reformation Church must – in order to keep in touch, if not with God, then with the times, and with temporal power – both enact and deny in its enacting.

Epilogue

> She bathed his Jobbernol thrice in the Fountain; then threw a handful of Meal on his Phyz ... caused him to take three little leaps, and to bump his A--- seven times against the ground, repeating I don't know what kind of Conjurations all the while in the *Toscan* [this should read Etruscan] tongue, and ever and anon reading in a *Ritual*, or Book of Ceremonies, carried after her by one of her *Mystagogues*.

Du Blioul's mystagogue is the newest of the mediatory characters introduced in narratives of pilgrimage to early modern Jerusalem. Where he got him from is unclear, though he may be a version of himself when no longer a literal pilgrim. For Du Blioul stayed on in Jerusalem for a time, served as chaplain to the Venetian trading community in Aleppo, and then returned to Besançon, where he became a famously cantankerous polemicist and recluse, countering – like his mystagogue – the attacks of Reformers both within and without the church. Like the mystagogue, he grew to be an old and learned man. It could be that his learning and his concern for style lead him to read Cicero's *Verrine Orations* (II, 59 § 132), and to translate the Latin mystagogues of Syracuse 'who act as guides to visitors, and show them the various things worth seeing' (Cicero 1935: 440) into his own guides around Jerusalem and through the meanings of Christian pilgrimage. If so, then the transposition of characters from Syracuse to Jerusalem is ironically appropriate for, as Cicero complains, the mystagogues have, owing to the pillage of certain imperial antique hunters, 'had to reverse the form of their explanations. Formerly, they showed you everywhere what things were; now they try to explain everywhere what has been taken away' (1935:441).

But there is also another, teasing possibility, which is that Du Blioul got his vernacular mystagogue from an altogether different kind of place. It is – just – possible, that he knew of the first mention of the term in French print, and indeed the only one to be cited in early dictionaries before it disappeared for centuries. The text in question is that quoted above at the start of this epilogue. It is from chapter forty-three of Rabelais' *Fifth Book*, in Urquhart's slightly bowdlerised, minimally inaccurate, but powerfully evocative translation recently reissued by Everyman (Rabelais 2000:797–98). The possibility is teasing, because it might be thought unlikely reading for the recluse in the Besançon seminary. The ritual Rabelais writes of takes place not in the Jerusalem of our pilgrims, nor yet in Cicero's Syracuse, but at the gates of the Temple of the Holy Bottle; the pilgrim is Panurge, and the mystagogues are women. But theirs is another story.

Acknowledgements

I have explored aspects of the argument developed here in papers given in the French Department at the University of Bangor and at the 'Travel and Nation' conference at the British Academy. I am grateful to the organisers of both events for the opportunity to try the readings out, and to respondents for comments. I am especially grateful to both Simon Coleman and Jas Elsner for their stimulating comments on this piece. They have proved exemplary editors.

References

I have given only short titles here, have given neither publishers nor library shelfmarks of early modern books, and have used modern translations and editions where they exist; otherwise, all translations in the text are mine.

Balourdet, L. (1601) *La Guide des chemins pour le Voyage de Hierusalem et autres villes et lieux de la Terre saincte*. Chalons.

de Beauvau, H. (1608) *Relation journaliere du voyage du Levant*. Toul.

―――― (1615) *Relation journaliere du voyage du Leuant. Reueu augmenté et enrichy par l'autheur de pourtraicts des lieux le plus remarquables*. Nancy.

de Castela, H. (1603), *Le Sainct voyage de Hierusalem et Mont Sinay faict en l'an du grand Jubilé*. Bordeaux.

―――― (1604) *La Guide et Adresse pour ceux qui veullent faire le S. voyage de Hierusalem*. Paris.

Cicero, M. T. (1935) *Verrine Orations*, ed. and trans. L.H.G. Greenwood. London and Cambridge, M.A.: Loeb Classical Library.

Du Blioul, J. (1599) *Hierosolymitanae Peregrinationis Hodoeporicon. Septem dialogorum libris explicatum*. Cologne.

―――― (1602) *Le Voyage de Hierusalem, et Pelerinage des saints lieux de la Palestine*. Besançon.

Giraudet, G. (1575) *Discours du Voyage d'Outre-Mer au S. Sepulchre de Jerusalem et autres lieux de la Terre Saincte*. Lyon.

Gomez-Géraud, M.-C. (1987) 'La Figure de l'interprète dans quelques récits de voyage français à la Renaissance', in J. Céard and J-C Margolin (eds), *Voyager à la Renaissance, Actes du Colloque de Tours 30 juin–12 juillet 1983*. Paris: Maisonneuve et Larose.

―――― (2000) *Le Crépuscule du Grand Voyage: Les récits des pèlerins à Jérusalem (1458–1612)*. Paris: Honoré Champion.

de Hault, N. (1601) *Le Voyage de Hierusalem fait l'an mil cinq cens quatre vingts treize*. Paris.

Le Huen, N. (1488) *Des Sainctes Peregrinations de Jherusalem et des anvirons et des lieux prochains*. Lyon.

de Léry, J. (1992) *Histoire d'un Voyage fait en la terre du Brésil – 1557 – (édition de 1580)*, ed. F. Lestringant. Montpellier: Presses du Languedoc.

―――― (1990) *History of a Voyage to the Land of Brazil, Otherwise called America*, ed. and trans. J. Whatley. Berkeley, Los Angeles and Oxford: University of California Press.

Maraval, P. (1986) 'Une querelle sur les pèlerinages autour d'un texte patristique (Grégoire de Nysse, lettre 2)', *Revue d'Histoire et de Philosophie Religieuses*, 66, 2: 131–41.

Paviot, J. (1987) 'Autour de l'ambassade de D'Aramon: érudits et voyageurs au Levant, 1547–1553', in *Voyager à la Renaissance. Actes du Colloque de Tours 30 juin–12 juillet 1983*. Paris: Maisonneuve et Larose.

Rabelais, F. (2000) *Gargantua and Pantagruel*, trans. P. Le Motteux and T. Urquhart, and ed. T.C. Cave. London: Everyman J. M. Dent.

Regnaut, A. (1573) *Discours du voyage d'Outre-Mer*. Lyons.

Savary de Brèves, F (1628) *Relation des Voyages de M. de Breues, tant en Grece, Terre-*

Saincte, et Aegypte, qu'aux royaumes de Tunis & Arger. Ensemble un Traicté faict l'an 1604, entre le Roy Henry le Grand & l'Empereur des Turcs et trois Discours du dit Sieur. Le tout recueilly par le S[ieur] D[u] C[astel], Paris.

────── (1787) 'Catalogue des manscrits apportés du Levant par ... De Brèves', in J. de Guignes, *Essai historique sur la typographie Orientale et Grecque*. Paris.

Tinguely, F. (2000) *L'Écriture du Levant à la Renaissance: Enquête sur les voyageurs français dans l'empire de Soliman le Magnifique*. Geneva: Droz.

Williams, W. (1999a) 'Rubbing up Against Others: Montaigne on Pilgrimage', in J. Elsner and J-P. Rubiés (eds) *Voyages and Visions: Towards a Cultural History of Travel*. London: Reaktion Books.

────── (1999b) *Pilgrimage and Narrative in the French Renaissance: 'The Undiscovered Country'*. Oxford: Clarendon Press.

────── (2000) '"Strange Fruit": The Culture of Pilgrimage from Mandeville to the Missionaries', in G.H. Tucker (ed.) *Forms of the "Medieval" in the "Renaissance"*. Charlottesville: Rookwood Press.

Pilgrimage into Words and Images: the Miracles of Santa Maria delle Carceri in Renaissance Prato

Robert Maniura
Birkbeck College, London

On 6 July 1484 an eight-year-old boy called Jacopino was chasing a cricket in the derelict area of Prato near the old castle when he saw the figure of the Virgin Mary, painted above a barred window of the ruined town prison (Figure. 1), 'detach itself' from the wall. The Virgin, who had been holding her son in her arms, placed him on the ground and, leaving him wriggling at the foot of the window, descended into the prison vaults. She proceeded to clean the place, 'scrubbing three times with her hand', before collecting her son and resuming her place on the wall. The boy hurried home to tell his mother what he had seen, but she would have none of it. She scolded him for his truancy and sent him back to school. Instead of returning to school, however, the boy returned to gaze at the image 'as if in ecstasy'. His rapt attention drew others to the site and the image was seen to undergo further miraculous transformations: the figure of the Virgin cried, opened and closed its eyes and sweated blood. The questioning of the boy by the vicar of the bishop of Pistoia, in whose diocese Prato lay, served to draw even more notice and crowds began to gather in anticipation of further wonders.

This detailed account of the origin of the cult of Santa Maria delle Carceri – Saint Mary of the Prison – in Prato survives in a manuscript written in 1505 by a Pratese lawyer, Giuliano di Francesco Guizzelmi (G. Guizzelmi 1505: fols. 8v–12v; Davies 1992: 397–400). The image on the prison wall quickly established a reputation for healing miracles as well as spectacular visual effects, and by the time Guizzelmi was writing the site had become a significant pilgrimage destination with a splendid

Figure 1 Virgin and Child with Sts Stephen and Leonard. Fourteenth-century wall painting venerated as *Santa Maria delle Carceri*. Basilica of Santa Maria delle Carceri, Prato. Photo: Soprintendenza per i Beni Architettonici e per il Paesaggio per le Provincie di Firenze, Pistoia e Prato.

new church, designed by Giuliano da Sangallo, to enshrine the precious picture (Morselli and Corti 1982; Davies 1993,1995). The story of Jacopino's ecstatic experience serves explicitly to affirm the holiness of the place and to act as a ground for the flourishing cult. It rationalises the appeal of this particular image. As with many origin myths of pilgrimage sites, there is a tension between the narrative and the experience it describes. The boy's story is said to have been discounted initially, but this denial is exploited in a topos of steadfast truth-telling in a later written account not authored by the boy.

In fact, Jacopino plays a relatively minor role in Guizzelmi's book. Having validated the 'specialness' of the place, he makes no further appearance. The bulk of the manuscript's seventy-eight folios comprises accounts of ninety-four of the further miracles associated with the shrine, dated between summer 1484 and April 1488. It is the pilgrims who form the focus of the book.

Such a retrospective collection of material, celebrating the origins and efficacy of an established holy place, sits comfortably in a long literary tradition of *miracula*. Recognition of the genre, however, by no means exhausts the significance of the text. For all its debt to convention, Guizzelmi's book represents an invaluable source for the study of pilgrimage. Its value lies in the insight it affords into the process of turning pilgrimage into words. Most pilgrims did not, and could not, write about their experiences. Detailed accounts of individual pilgrim journeys are exceptional. Yet miracle collections are common and in miracle collections, as I will argue, the very stuff of pilgrimage becomes the raw material for a writer. In Guizzelmi's case we happen to know a good deal about both the writer and the early history of the shrine with which he deals. The survival of Guizzelmi's own diary-cum-account-books, or *memoriale* (G. Guizzelmi 1488–1518), his biography by one of his descendants, Agostino Guizzelmi (A. Guizzelmi 1597), and an earlier collection of Carceri miracles (Germanino 1487) allows us to ask detailed questions about the writing of his miracle collection. I will use the miracle stories in Guizzelmi's manuscript as a starting-point for an exploration of the transformation of pilgrimage into writing.

That process of transformation must be conceived of as involving much more than the compositional decisions of an individual author. We are dealing with successive writings and rewritings. This becomes clear as soon as we compare Guizzelmi's book to the only other surviving collection of miracles of the Carceri shrine, a manuscript entitled 'Miracoli et gratie della gloriosa Madre Vergine Maria Delle Charcere di Prato Lanno MCCCCLXXXIIII', preserved as codex 86 in the *Biblioteca Roncioniana* in Prato (Germanino 1487). This text is sometimes attributed to a certain Andrea del Germanino, as will be discussed below, and has been dated to shortly after 1487 (Bandini 1984: 56). The text is in three parts. The first consists of a numbered sequence of 179 miracle stories, largely, but not exclusively, healing miracles, arranged in chronological order. The second part is presented as a list of the miraculous transformations of the image but also contains what amounts to a chronicle of the shrine's early history. The third part contains a list of processions undertaken to the shrine. Parts two and three have been published (Bandini 1984: 60–96). The first part of the text treats the same theme as Guizzelmi's collection and, unsurprisingly, there is a significant overlap in content: forty-five of Guizzelmi's ninety-four miracle stories duplicate stories found in the earlier volume. The bulk of the duplicated miracles form a more or less continuous block appearing at the start of both manuscripts. To be precise, of the first thirty-eight miracle stories in codex 86, thirty-six appear among the first forty-two miracles in Guizzelmi's book. With respect to this material Guizzelmi emerges as no more than an editor.

Codex 86 is, however, unlikely to have been Guizzelmi's direct source for the stories he duplicates. His wording of the duplicated stories, though very close to that of codex 86, is seldom identical, but that could just be a desire to avoid appearing a slavish copyist. More importantly, the dates he gives to some of the duplicated miracles differ. To give but one example, the first fifteen of Guizzelmi's miracles reproduce all but one of the first sixteen given in the earlier manuscript. Miracle number 11 of the latter is omitted. They appear in the same sequence and bear the same dates, the final miracle of the group dated 1 August 1484 in both collections. Guizzelmi's next three miracles are all also said to have occurred on this date. But his sixteenth miracle story reproduces that which appears in the earlier manuscript as number 34 where it is dated 1 September. His seventeenth and eighteenth miracles appear as numbers 25 and 26 in the earlier text, where they are dated to 8 August. The reordering of the stories does not result in any gain in coherence in presentation or reveal any overt attempt to structure the material, and it is difficult to construe the discrepancy as the result of a conscious editorial adjustment. We could hypothesise that codex 86 represented what Guizzelmi regarded as a 'corrupt' source, which he attempted to 'correct' on the basis of some other authority. But it seems more likely that both manuscripts draw on a further text or texts in which at least some of the miracle stories were undated. In either case the surviving Carceri miracle collections are revealed as no more than fragments of the writing process.

A brief review of the structure of codex 86 helps to reveal just how extended that process was. The collection of miracles constituting the first section can itself be broken down in into at least three parts. The first part comprises those stories in large part reproduced by Guizzelmi. Their very duplication reveals the relatively wide diffusion of this group and, as I have suggested elsewhere, they may reflect the content of a miracle collection, perhaps printed, distributed by the shrine's custodians. Some of the later stories in codex 86 refer to just such a pamphlet (Maniura forthcoming). The two other parts claim to derive from specific sources. The stories numbered from 39 to 109 contain a phrase to the effect that the story was told or notified to the people assembled at the shrine 'by frate Agostino', who is identified as 'the chaplain of that place' (e.g. Germanino 1487: No. 39, fol. 8v). A further group, beginning with miracle 130 and continuing until the end of the numbered sequence, is presented as taken from 'the book of Andrea del Germanino', specified as he 'who sells the candles', and giving precise folio references (e.g. Germanino 1487: No. 130, fol. 29r). The appearance of these two names in the text as figures who recorded or announced miracles has prompted attributions of the manuscript itself to one or the other (Guasti 1844: 158; Bandini 1984: 56). There is, however, no compelling reason to suppose that either actually produced the surviving manuscript. The significant point is rather that the text reaches beyond itself to indicate yet more sources.

We are in danger here of becoming caught in a philological hall of mirrors: a never-ending chain of putative sources. Rather than pursuing some illusory ur-text, therefore, let us change direction and consider the further development of the collection in Guizzelmi's hands. The analysis will help to clarify that, in respect of miracle stories, the source or origin has to be sought elsewhere than in a textual model. Not only does Guizzelmi's book include a substantial number of miracles which are not found in any other surviving collection, but some of the stories implicitly claim an originary status. In the latter part of his book the stories cease to be remote third-person narratives and become entwined with Guizzelmi's own concerns and, finally, his own experience.

The development is almost imperceptible at first. The subject of his forty-first story, dated 15 September 1484, is introduced, without comment, as 'Francesco d'Andrea di Francesco Ghuççelmi of Prato, a boy of two years and eight months' (G. Guizzelmi 1505: fol. 33v). The child had suffered from a fever for two days and had neither eaten nor drunk anything in that time. Only in the middle of the story does Guizzelmi's interest become explicit: 'Andrea, his father and my brother, went to the Madonna delle Carceri and there vowed him to her Majesty'. The story is one of three in the collection involving members of Guizzelmi's close family. In his eighty-seventh story one of his brothers, Raphaello, is cured of a tumour, having vowed to the Virgin of the Carceri to become a priest (G. Guizzelmi 1505: fols. 64v–65v). In the eighty-eighth another nephew, Lactantio d'Andrea, a baby of just eight months, is cured of epilepsy when the writer himself, Giuliano, vows him to the shrine (G. Guizzelmi 1505: fols. 65v–67r). The climax of this direct personal and emotional investment comes in the seventy-second story, in which Giuliano attributes to the Virgin of the Carceri his own avoidance of injury when kicked by a mule on the way back from Borgo Sansepolcro (G. Guizzelmi 1505: fols. 57v–58v).

Guizzelmi's role in these stories is not confined to those in which the miraculous outcome is a matter of personal interest. He also appears as a character in a number of other stories, where he plays the role of an active promoter of the cult. He exploits his peripatetic legal career to act as a kind of roving ambassador for the shrine, telling people of the miracles of the Virgin of the Carceri and urging them to make a vow. 'Do you have a devotion to the Madonna of the Carceri?' he asks a boy in Bologna, bleeding profusely from the nose, in the last story in the collection; 'Commend yourself to Her Majesty and say a Pater Noster and an Ave Maria.' He does not rely solely on verbal exhortation. In this story he takes from his bag a 'Madonna in lead, made in the similitude of the Madonna delle Carceri' and says 'Look at this. This is the Madonna of Prato. Commend yourself to her with a good heart' (G. Guizzelmi 1505: fols. 71v–72r).

Guizzelmi places considerable stress on his distribution of Carceri pilgrim tokens. He has himself giving away 'figures' of the Madonna in lead or on paper in seven other stories in the collection (G. Guizzelmi 1505: fols. 35v, 36r–v, 39v, 42v, 49r, 52r–v, 66r). Indeed, he presents himself as a well-known purveyor of such objects. Ser Davino, the procurator of Pisa, comes to ask him for 'a Virgin Mary which had touched the Madonna delle Carceri' to place around the neck of a dangerously ill woman (G. Guizzelmi 1505: fol. 42v). In most cases the gift of the image is presented as the very catalyst of miracle. As soon as Guizzelmi hangs such an image around the neck of the gangrenous Gabriello di Matteo di Gabriello of Pistoia the sick man begins to recover and exclaims: 'Messer Giuliano, you have healed me' (G. Guizzelmi 1505: fol. 52v). None of the lead images seems to have survived but at least one of the images on paper does. A very worn woodcut, closely following the iconography of the Carceri painting, is preserved, stuck to the piece of reused parchment which now forms the flyleaf of Guizzelmi's miracle book (Figure 2). It may be an example of one of the prints Guizzelmi himself distributed.

I will have reason to return to Guizzelmi's strategies as a propagator of the cult of the Carceri but at this point we need to consider the significance of these first-person interventions. We need to be aware that Guizzelmi, as a prominent professional man, had been directly involved in the administration of the shrine, having served a term in 1503–4 as a member of the *opera* or lay building committee of the new church (Archivio di Stato di Prato: fol.10v; G. Guizzelmi 1488–1518: fol. 163v; A. Guizzelmi 1597: fol. 20r). It is tempting to see his miracle book as a textual component of a broader process of articulation of the shrine, incorporating both the elaboration of its miraculous history and its immediate built environment; an element of the 'landscape' of the shrine in the terms proposed by Coleman and Elsner (1995: 212). Is the book any more than a piece of promotional material from a loyal one-time servant of the *opera*?

Guizzelmi openly presents himself in his text as a promoter of the shrine but we need to be careful not to prejudge his possible intentions.

Figure 2 Santa Maria delle Carceri. Woodcut. Late fifteenth century. Photo: Biblioteca Roncioniana, Prato.

In particular we should not fall into the trap of assuming that those who are actively involved in fashioning the landscape of a pilgrimage shrine somehow stand outside the system. In the case of Guizzelmi we can show that he explicitly shared the conceptual framework of those who came on pilgrimage to the Virgin of the Carceri. In the strict sense he never was, and never could be, a pilgrim to Prato. He lived there. But he was a pilgrim. He notes in his *memoriale* the lodgement of his will with Niccolò de' Bardi, guardian of the Franciscan friary of the Palco, near Prato on 28 April 1499, in consequence of his vow to visit 'the Holy Land and the most Holy Sepulchre of our Lord Jesus Christ' (G. Guizzelmi 1488–1518: fol. 128r). His biographer implies that his vow was prompted by his ambiguous part in the conviction and execution of an innocent man when he was acting as a judge in Arezzo (A. Guizzelmi 1597: fol. 16v; G. Guizzelmi 1990: 23). In the event he never reached Jerusalem. He set out from Prato on 8 May 1499 but only got as far as Venice. A 'great Turkish army' blocked the route and he was forced to turn back. Ironically, his attempted pilgrimage made him seriously ill. He languished for several months in Bologna on his way back, finally arriving home only on 20 October. In his *memoriale* he ruefully records that altogether the abortive trip cost him thirty-six Venetian gold ducats (G. Guizzelmi 1488–1518: fol. 129v). The seriousness of his undertaking was not forgotten, however. Agostino Guizzelmi records that the priest anointing Giuliano's body on his deathbed in 1518 found fragments of a hair shirt embedded in his flesh. He had worn it ever since he had failed to satisfy the pilgrimage vow he had made nineteen years earlier (A. Guizzelmi 1597: fols. 31v–32r; G. Guizzelmi 1990: 32).

Guizzelmi's frequent changes of location for his work also placed him in a position to make undertakings directly analogous to pilgrimage vows with respect to the holy places of his native city. Agostino tells us that during his first posting to Castigtlion Fiorentino in 1480–1 the young lawyer fell ill and vowed to place a wax image of himself before the 'large Crucifix' in the *pieve*, now the cathedral, of Prato if he recovered (A. Guizzelmi 1597: fols. 7v–9r). In his day this crucifix, a large-scale Romanesque sculpture which was dismembered and dispersed in the nineteenth century (Marchini 1963: 47–53), was associated with copious miracles. Guizzelmi himself wrote a collection of miracles associated with the object. This work, now lost, was complete by 1496, when the writer first recorded his loan of the book in his *memoriale* (G. Guizzelmi 1488–1518: fol. 103v). It is suggestive that Agostino mentions the miracle book in his treatment of Giuliano's vow. Like his votive offering, the book was a testament to Guizzelmi's devotion. We should allow that Guizzelmi's writing of the Carceri miracles too was as much a devotional as a promotional exercise.

Guizzelmi's concluding remarks address his text to a generalised posterity (G. Guizzelmi 1488–1518: fols. 77v–78r), but in considering the status of his book we should be aware that it gained very little diffusion. The text remains unpublished and, as far as I am aware, it survives only in the single autograph manuscript copy in the *Biblioteca Roncioniana*. Agostino notes that in his day a book of Carceri miracles written by Giuliano was preserved in the family house (A. Guizzelmi 1597: fol. 6r). This may have been the volume now in the *Roncioniana*. A detail of the book's current physical make-up supports the idea. The current binding is modern but pieces of reused parchment serve as end papers for the nine gatherings of paper on which the main body of the book is written. As we have seen, a print bearing a reproduction of the holy image is pasted to that at the start of the manuscript. The verso of the piece of parchment at the end of the volume bears a very selective index. The date of these insertions is difficult to ascertain but the index is written in two hands which are plausibly sixteenth century in date. This index lists six miracles and gives their folio references in the manuscript. Three of the miracles listed are the Guizzelmi family miracles noted above and a further story listed, which duplicates one in codex 86, relates to a certain 'Cosimo di Lorenzo di Butone' who, in Giuliano's text, is also surnamed Guizzelmi. The family focus is explicit. Giuliano Guizzelmi's Carceri miracle book long had a very restricted audience. If this book can be regarded as part of the landscape of the shrine, it is as a part of the landscape with the narrowest of horizons.

The significance of Giuliano's miracle book for this family audience is revealed when we learn that the fragments of the hair shirt mentioned above were also kept in the house (A. Guizzelmi 1597: fol. 31v). These mementos occupy the boundary between heirloom and relic and, together with the book which records their preservation, begin to generate a form of family hagiography. Giuliano Guizzelmi's descendants clearly regarded him as, at the very least, a notably pious man. This informs our reading of his text. Whether or not he intended large-scale distribution of his Carceri book, we must allow that the first-person interjections in his text are motivated by something other than purely rhetorical considerations. This book was important to him. We can freely acknowledge that his writing draws on the established literary genre of miracle collections. The conventional structures are, however, employed to articulate something about Guizzelmi's experience of the world. They give him the words but the stories are traces of something beyond the text. Giuliano would not have seen himself as an author in a modern sense.

This consideration of Guizzelmi's interests in the writing of these explicitly new stories can help with our reading of the rewritten stories whose authors we do not know. I propose that they are all traces of something beyond the text: they are traces of pilgrimage. Let us consider one of them. Take the following, which appears as the eighteenth story in Guizzelmi's collection (G. Guizzelmi 1505: fol. 20r). It repeats very closely the story found as number 26 in codex 86 (Germanino 1487: fols. 5v–6r):

On this day, 1 August 1484, Martino di Domenico da Calenzano in the vicinity of Florence, a boy of 10, broke his left leg and it healed badly so that he could not walk without crutches. His father vowed, promising, if the boy was healed, to place a leg made of wax at this glorious Madonna and leave the crutches. Having made the vow the boy was immediately healed and afterwards on the 8th they fulfilled the vow.

It would be misleading to nominate any single story as wholly 'typical' but the tale of Martino di Domenico can be taken as representative of many in two crucial respects: its extreme brevity and its basic narrative structure. A person in distress vows to visit the shrine, perceives the granting of divine aid and makes the visit, leaving behind a material token. This simple structure is of profound importance. It deals with the very building blocks of pilgrimage: the vow and the journey. Pilgrimage in the Christian tradition is the very antithesis of casual travel. However one wishes to characterise its goal – 'holy place' or 'realm of competing discourses' (Eade and Sallnow 1991) – pilgrimage presupposes a specific undertaking: to go to a 'different place' (Dubisch 1995). These stories display an acute awareness of precisely the solemnity of the undertaking and the significance of place – the distinction between here and there, home and shrine. The writer himself was a Prato resident and not a Prato pilgrim but, as we have seen, he too was familiar with this essential conceptual leap across space. The very raw material of pilgrimage is captured between these unassuming lines.

How can this be? How does pilgrimage get caught up in writing? The leg made of wax and the crutches in the story of Martino di Domenico help to formulate the issue. Altogether forty-four of the stories in Guizzelmi's collection refer to material votive offerings. These votive offerings can help to conceptualise the way pilgrimage can leave traces. Some of the offerings are donations in kind such as livestock, cloth and precious metal which were commonly sold to generate cash. Others are donations of consumables such as candles or wax. But no fewer than twenty-five stories refer to offerings of images intended to be displayed at the shrine. The bulk are made of wax. A number, like Martino's wax leg, figure diseased or injured body parts but many represent the whole figure of the donor or vowed person, sometimes explicitly life-size. Guizzelmi himself donated a life-sized silver-covered wax figure of his nephew Lactantio as part of the vow noted above (G. Guizzelmi 1505: fol. 66v). The cost of the figure, placed in the church in December 1488, is duly noted in his *memoriale* (G. Guizzelmi 1488–1518: fols. 2v–3r). None of these notoriously friable objects survive at the church of Santa Maria delle Carceri but we must imagine the clean lines of Sangallo's architecture complicated by a fulsome array of wax votive images analogous to those which once famously crowded the shrine of the Santissima Annunziata in Florence (Morselli 1985; Warburg 1999: 204–8). Such votive offerings both visualised the vow and recorded its fulfilment by physically marking the shrine on or after the pilgrim's arrival. Votive offerings are unambiguously traces of individual pilgrim journeys. I propose that the miracle stories themselves are the fragmentary textual equivalents of votive offerings: written traces of pilgrimage.

The relationship I wish to evoke between a laconic text and an otherwise irrecoverable journey can perhaps be drawn out by analogy with some of the works of the British landscape artist Richard Long. Long has produced performances which consist of extensive journeys through landscape but with the exhibition component of the work reduced to a very brief written account of the route taken. The viewer is invited to contemplate the plenitude of the artist's experience of landscape whilst gazing at a few printed words. The reader of the Carceri miracles need not engage with the pointed comment upon the British landscape tradition but should be aware of the possible relationship between textual marks and elaborate performance.

In the story of Martino di Domenico there is, of course, a gap between the pilgrim's performance and the text. Unlike Guizzelmi in his stories of miracles in which he was involved, or Long in his written landscapes, neither the subject of the miracle nor one close to him is the writer. The same is true of the majority of stories in any miracle collection. Pilgrim authorship, in the sense of actual inscription, of miracle narratives is exceptional. It is highlighted as such in Guizzelmi's text. Maestro Dianoro di Paolo di Ser Mattheo of Viterbo, a Dominican friar, is singled out as someone who both preached about his own miraculous cure and wrote an account of it 'in his own hand'. Guizzelmi's text claims to include a transcription of Maestro Dianoro's testimony, written 'in a book of this Virgin Mary' (G. Guizzelmi 1505: fols. 29r–32v). But pilgrims can be tellers of stories and it is on this level that miracle narrative and votive offering can be seen to be closely related. Pilgrims arriving at a shrine brought their experiences with them and could articulate and celebrate them in a number of ways. The purchase and donation of a votive offering was one way. Verbal announcement was another. It is not unreasonable to suppose that someone who believed themselves delivered from a serious illness or injury would want to tell people about it. Loud and sustained public proclamation of the miraculous is indeed a feature of a number of stories in these collections. Mona Catherina from Querceto suffered from severe pains in her arms and when they disappeared on gazing at the image of the Virgin of the Carceri on 22 August 1484 she drew attention to the miracle 'in a loud voice' (Germanino 1487: fol. 7r; G. Guizzelmi 1505: fol. 27v). The telling, like the physical offering, also acts as a form of gift; a performance of thanksgiving. The gap arises at the point at which those stories are transformed into written text. This is a critical nexus and one to which I will return. I wish to note here, however, that there is no need to mystify the process by which the gap is filled. The clergy and officers of the *opera* on site, the chaplain and the candle seller so frequently mentioned in codex 86, are eminently plausible candidates for the initial recorders of pilgrim announcements and it is unsurprising that the custodians of a shrine should want to record them. Perhaps they did make an immediate note of the stories in a kind of systematic ledger of miracles and such a record is presumably the 'book of the Virgin' referred to in the story of Maestro Dianoro. It is significant that Domenico from Calenzano did not himself write the story of his son's healing but we need not doubt the reality of his short journey from Calenzano to Prato. The journey is the ultimate 'source' of the story.

To call the initial writers of the miracles 'recorders' is not to downplay the importance of writing itself nor to deny the necessary transformations that it brings to what gets written down. In the Carceri miracle books we have an intriguing instance, which demonstrates the mutability of lived experience at the hands of writers. We have what appear to be two independent written accounts of the same 'miracle'; stories in each of the two surviving collections, that is, which appear to deal with the same series of events but which appear not have a common written source. The story is one of those in which Guizzelmi claims to have been directly involved as a distributor of pilgrim tokens. It is worth relating the two versions of the story at length. Guizzelmi has the following:

> The month of May 1485. Mona Antonia, once wife of Mariano di Michele from Vico Pisano and mother of Ser Jacopo di Mariano from Vico, procurator of Pisa, suffered from and was incapacitated by certain pains which she had in both feet so that for the space of eight months she could not walk without crutches. I gave Ser Jacopo, her son, a figure of Saint Mary of the Prison which had touched the most glorious figure of Saint Mary of the Prison of Prato and I said that he should take this to his mother and that it would comfort her, if she were to vow with a good heart to the said most glorious Virgin Mary of the Prison and that she would see miracles. The said Ser Jacopo took this figure to the said Mona Antonia his mother with devotion. She vowed, promising to stay a month without eating meat in reverence of

the most Glorious Virgin Mary. And the following day she left one crutch and on the third day the other and she was healed through the grace of the most Glorious Virgin Mary in the month of May 1485. I was at that time the judge of the *podestà* of Pisa. The said Ser Jacopo, her son, told me all this with great rejoicing, telling me that his mother wanted to go to Prato to visit the most Glorious Virgin by whom she was liberated. (G. Guizzelmi 1505: fols. 35v–36r)

Codex 86 has this between two stories dated 24 and 26 June 1485:

82: After compline the said Frate Agostino told how Mona Piera di Mariano di Michele da Vico in the contado of Pisa was in Pisa when she developed an illness of the legs which lasted for about eight years walking only with two crutches from the bed to the fire. She tried many medicines and went to baths but nothing helped her. Messer Giuliano di Bachino was then a judge in Pisa with the *podestà* or rather captain and this woman had a son called Ser Antonio who was a procurator in that place who was worried about his mother and this said illness. The said Messer Giuliano said to him I will give you a good medicine for your mother's illness saying take one of these painted Virgin Marys of which I have a few and a book of miracles and have your mother vow to this figure and you vow her also. And the one and the other having made this vow she began to walk with one crutch and following her devotion and her vow in a few days she was healed through the grace received. (Germanino 1487: fols. 17r–v)

The two stories share a basic outline. A woman from Vico Pisano, whose son is a procurator in Pisa, and who is only able to walk with crutches, is healed on making a vow prompted by an image of Santa Maria delle Carceri given to her by 'Messer Giuliano'. But the details differ. The names change. Giuliano Guizzelmi becomes Giuliano di Bachino. The mother in one story bears the name assigned to her son in the other. In one case the woman's illness has lasted for eight months and in the other for eight years. There can be little doubt, however, that both accounts are attempting to tell the same story. Guizzelmi is not necessarily the more accurate despite his privileged information. He was, after all, writing about events that were meant to have taken place some twenty years earlier. Data capture is never a neutral process.

The terminology of information technology suggests a helpful analogy. The writing process in miracle collections often seems to be little more than the insertion of data in the fields of a database: date, name, place of origin and illness, injury or injustice suffered. We should not assume, however, that such structures are necessarily imposed upon the pilgrims from without. The chaplain and the candle seller, if they did write miracles down, were just as much part of a conceptual landscape shared with the pilgrims as we have seen Guizzelmi was. Vow and journey are simply what pilgrimage was conceived to consist in. The idea of the custodians of the shrine ticking pilgrims off on some kind of preprinted conceptual form is true to the process. This image of the writers of miracle stories as 'mark makers' captures the very essence of the miracle story as written journey. The writing, like the votive offering, marks the conclusion of the journey from here to there. The journey to the shrine occupies the space between the making of the vow and its inscription in the miracle book. It is in this light that we should see the apparent instability of the stories revealed in the above example. It is the 'mark' that matters. Like the votive offerings, the stories need not be reliable sources of biographical information.

The journey so captured gives little sense of movement through either time or space. Few of the stories actually register the pains or pleasures, perhaps one might say the distractions, of travel itself. This might seem disappointing, but it is very significant. The experience of geographical space is collapsed into a matrix in which the only spatial terms are the points of departure and the common point of arrival. This is a familiar convention: it is the language of the airport or railway station arrivals board. The analogy with modern, high-speed, high-technology travel is productive. The arrivals board, another overlooked form of travel writing perhaps, says as much about most modern journeys as many travellers would want to. In the end the quality or duration of the travel experience is secondary. To have arrived is everything. The miracle stories suggest that the same is true of pilgrimage. Travelling hopefully counts for very little. Consider again Guizzelmi's frustrated attempt to reach the Holy Land. He made the effort and undertook a journey, but in a fundamental sense it did not count.

The lack of physical definition in the journey itself can be expressed in another way. Analyses of miracle collections often take advantage of the detailed specification of points of pilgrim origin to map the catchment area of a shrine. Such scatter diagrams help to reinforce the physical reality of these economically written journeys but they are in a sense misleading. We would like to be able to join the scattered points of origin to the shrine to trace a series of individual pilgrim itineraries. But we are unable to do this on what, according to current conventions, we regard as a topographically accurate map. We have no way of reliably reconstructing the paths followed. In as far as we can produce a map from miracle stories it is a topological one, like the map of the London Underground, where we can see the relative positions of points of origin to the shrine but where neither size nor shape, and hence neither distance nor precise route, is recorded.

In as far as the journeys themselves do emerge at all in the miracle stories it is not in terms of physical movement but as an ambiguous conceptual space full of uncertainty, where the pilgrim faces troubling challenges. Mona Catherina from Querceto, whom we met above shouting out her miracle, had 'heard it said on the road that Saint Mary of the Prison no longer worked miracles and that her journey was in vain' (Germanino 1487: fol. 7r; G. Guizzelmi 1505: fol. 27v). Her strident declaration at the shrine triumphantly articulates her justification in persevering with the journey. Another case constitutes an explicit piece of holy competition. Ser Nicolò, rector of Santa Lucia alla Pieve Vechia, was 'in the Marches on the way to S. Maria di Loreto', the preeminent Italian Marian shrine, in September 1485 when he fell ill. His companions, convinced that there was no hope, wanted to leave him but he vowed to visit Santa Maria delle Carceri barefoot and he recovered (G. Guizzelmi 1505: fol. 49v). Whether the priest had a vow to Loreto or whether he was a companion of one who did, the journey is clearly not just an occasion for physical hardship but also for hard decisions.

For all their tantalising brevity and selectivity, miracle stories occupy an important place in the writing of pilgrimage. They constitute a way in which the journeys of nonwriters, and hence the majority of pilgrims, can become fixed in text. Yet writing is clearly not the natural medium for a pilgrim discourse. I have suggested that we can easily see how the gap between pilgrimage and writing gets filled, but the gap remains. A votive offering may be an integral part of the pilgrimage. The decision to make an offering and the responsibility for its delivery lie with the pilgrim. The written story is, by contrast, usually wholly outside the pilgrim's control. The pilgrim may decide to announce his or her experience but cannot ensure that it is recorded and may have no interest in its recording. The miracle story is no more than a by-product of pilgrimage. The fugitive nature of the verbal testimony and the incompleteness of the written record in the face of the abundant material traces of pilgrimage is a theme taken up by Guizzelmi in the conclusion to his miracle book: 'This Most Glorious Madonna has worked, and still works every hour, many other miracles and signs both in the region of Prato and in many other places beyond it and I have recorded a large number, but because of negligence neither the names of those who have received graces nor the places nor times [are known] although they may have made large offerings and carried out their vows.' (G. Guizzelmi 1505: fol. 72r).

The pilgrims did not, however, lack a discourse of their own. It is simply that their discourse was not primarily written. It was conducted in visual images. We have already highlighted two vital components of this visual system: images as votive offerings and images as pilgrim tokens. The force of this nonverbal system is indicated by Guizzelmi's own miracle. His attribution of his miraculous avoidance of injury did not stem from the utterance of a specific vow. 'I recognized', he writes, 'the most glorious Virgin Mary of the Carceri in Prato, whose lead image ... I had on, to have preserved me unhurt ...' (G. Guizzelmi 1505: fol. 58r-v). The wearing of the image constituted a wordless vow.

One of the stories in codex 86 hints at the breadth of the system:

75: The said Frate Agostino told, on 29 May 1485, how Mariotto di Messer Giovanni de Vechi from San Gimignano, having had a great fever for about 50 days so that it seemed it would never leave him, was very ill and could find neither doctor nor medicine which could cure him. One day a relative said to him 'I will bring you a Virgin Mary of the Carceri from Prato. Commend yourself to her devoutly and perhaps grace will be granted to you'. And bringing him one of those figures of Our Lady on a piece of paper he commended himself devoutly to her, promising, if he was healed, to make an offering of an image in his similitude dressed all in purple. He vowed thus devoutly in bed and came here and satisfied his vow for grace received. (Germanino 1487: fol. 15r–v)

We should not forget what is only implicit here: that the centrepiece of this visual discourse was the holy picture itself. This image was the focus of the devotee's exchange with the saintly intercessor. The very goal of the pilgrim's journey to the Carceri was the sight of an image. This shrine image became the still centre of an ebb and flow of images. Mariotto's vow, in the above story, is prompted by an image of the shrine image of the Virgin. He marks its fulfilment and his thanks by placing an image of himself in the presence of the image of the saint. The richness and complexity of this process of visual exchange alerts us to the true extent and significance of the role of images in fifteenth-century religious practice. Part of the value of these brief textual records is the light they cast on this near-vanished, yet once extensive, mobilised body of visual material. The miracle stories are not only traces of pilgrimage but also of an entire visual culture.

It is perhaps ironic that what I have termed an incidental and inessential part of pilgrimage, the written word, should prove more durable than the images which I have claimed were the pilgrims' principal means of articulating their experiences. Yet this is perhaps not surprising. Pilgrim journeys became more or less accidentally inscribed in texts which were, however, concentrated at the still centre of the shrine. The images themselves undertook journeys, with the pilgrim tokens (Figure 2) dispersed to the pilgrims' points of origin and beyond, markers not of arrival but of return. This mobility of images, of course, made them a principal means of the dissemination of the shrine. But it also meant that images could come to inhabit that dangerous in-between place of the journey itself. Codex 86 has the story of Santi di Simone from Soglano who had suffered for several years from a tumour 'like an egg' in his leg. He remained in the hospital of Santa Maria Nuova in Florence for twenty-three months seeking a cure, and whilst there he heard of the miracles of the Carceri in Prato. He vowed to place there 'an image of his own size' and, with a group of companions, set off for Prato. On the way he felt his strength increase and the pain lessen so that he was able to dispense with one of his crutches. After about a mile 'they saw a piece of paper on an elm tree on which was this holy figure'. He commended himself with devotion and in a moment was liberated and healed and continued on his way to the Madonna without crutches (Germanino 1487: fol. 5r–v). Not only do images frame the journey, constituting both prompt and goal, they may also articulate it, guiding the pilgrim through the bewildering experience of travel. Pilgrimage is revealed as a journey through a landscape of images.

The miracle stories in Guizzelmi's collection need to be understood in the context of this broader network of signs. I set out to explore the transformation of pilgrimage into writing, a process I saw as transcending the decisions of any individual writer. The consideration of the written narratives alongside the material traces of pilgrimage helps to clarify this complex issue of authorship. In order to highlight the importance of the visual in pilgrim discourse in this period I stressed the gap between pilgrim experience and the inscription of the narrative of that experience, characterising the written story as a by-product of pilgrimage in contrast to the directly pilgrim-manipulated votive offering. In fact the distinction is not so sharp, for although a pilgrim may be responsible for the delivery of an offering, he or she is unlikely to be responsible for either its manufacture or its display. The pilgrim's offering is mediated by others, as is any story he or she may tell. The selection and disposition of *ex votos*, like the selection and inscription of miracle stories, represents a part of the transformation of pilgrim experience outside of the pilgrims' control. However, the contribution of the pilgrims which remains discernible in the material tokens shows that the trace of pilgrimage is not necessarily effaced in this transformation. Rather than seeing the miracle collections as static and self-contained literary constructs removed from the practice of pilgrimage, we should see them as part of a process of transformation initiated by the pilgrims themselves.

References

Archivio di Stato di Prato, Archivio Comunale, Diurnini, 112.

Bandini, L. (1984) 'Il quinto centenario della "mirabilissima apparitione"', *Archivio Storico Pratese* 60: 55–96.

Coleman, S. and Elsner, J. (1995) *Pilgrimage: Past and Present in the World Religions.* Cambridge, MA.: Harvard University Press.

Pilgrimage into Words and Images

Davies, P. (1992) 'Studies in the Quattrocento Centrally Planned Church'. PhD thesis, London University.

—— (1993) 'The Madonna delle Carceri in Prato and Italian Pilgrimage Architecture', *Architectural History* 36: 1–18.

—— (1995) 'The Early History of S. Maria delle Carceri in Prato', *Journal of the Society of Architectural Historians* 54, 3: 326–35.

Dubisch, J. (1995) *In a Different Place: Pilgrimage, Gender and Politics at a Greek Island Shrine*. Princeton: Princeton University Press.

Eade, J. and Sallnow, M. (eds) (1991) *Contesting the Sacred: the Anthropology of Christian Pilgrimage*. London: Routledge.

Germanino, A. del, (c.1487) 'Miracoli et gratie della gloriosa Madre Vergine Maria Delle Charcere di Prato Lanno MCCCCLXXXIIII'. Biblioteca Roncioniana, Prato. Codex 86.

[Guasti, C] (1844) *Bibliografia pratese compilata per un da Prato*. Prato: G. Pontecchi.

Guizzelmi, A., (c.1597) 'Vita di M. Giuliano di Francescho Guizzelmi fabricata da M. Agostino di Bindaccio Guizzelmi'. Archivio di Stato di Firenze, Ubaldini-Vai-Geppi 470.

Guizzelmi, G., (1488–1518) 'Memoriale'. Biblioteca Roncioniana, Prato. Codex 759.

—— (1505) 'Historia della Apparitione et Miracoli di Madonna Sancta Maria del Carcere di Prato'. Biblioteca Roncioniana, Prato. Codex 87.

—— (1990) *Historia della Cinctola della Vergine Maria*, ed. C. Grassi. Prato: Società Pratese di Storia Patria.

Maniura, R. (forthcoming) 'Image and Relic in the Cult of Our Lady of Prato', in S.J. Cornelison and S.B. Montgomery (eds) *Image, Relic and Devotion in Medieval and Renaissance Italy*. Tempe, Arizona: Medieval and Renaissance Texts and Studies.

Marchini, G. (1963) *Il Tesoro del Duomo di Prato*. Prato: Cassa di Risparmi e Depositi di Prato.

Morselli, P. (1985) 'Immagini di cera votive in S. Maria delle Carceri di Prato nella prima metà del '500', in A. Morragh, F. Superbi Gioffredi, P. Morselli and E. Borsook (eds) *Renaissance Studies in Honor of Craig Hugh Smyth*, II. Florence: Giunti Barbèra.

Morselli, P. and Corti, G. (1982) *La Chiesa di Santa Maria delle Carceri in Prato. Contributo di Lorenzo de' Medici e Giuliano da Sangallo alla progettazione*. Florence: EDAM.

Warburg, A. (1999) 'The Art of Portraiture and the Florentine Bourgeoisie', in *The Renewal of Pagan Antiquity*, trans. D. Britt. Los Angeles, CA.: Getty Research Institute: 185–22.

The Pilgrimage of Passion in Sidney's *Arcadia*

Helen Moore
Corpus Christi College, Oxford

Ai! car me fos lai peleris
Si qe mos fustz e mos tapis
Fos pelz sieus bels huoills remiratz!

[Ah! would that I were a pilgrim there
So that my staff and my cloak
Might be reflected in (beheld by) her beautiful eyes!

Jaufré Rudel, 'Lanquan li jorn son lonc en may', ll.33–35

Rudel's twelfth-century song, 'Lanquan li jorn son lonc en may', embodies the pain and longing of *amor de lonh*, or love from afar. The convention of *amor de lonh*, which originated in Provençal lyric poetry, stimulates the lover towards agonised introspection at the same time as impelling his thoughts outward, towards the distant object of his desire. This motif of the distant beloved means that Rudel's lyrics express love as a desire for travel: when the defining – indeed, only – feature of the beloved is her distance, desire and the impulse to travel become compacted together. In the thirteenth-century *Life* of Rudel (described by one editor as 'a narrative transformation and concretization of the dreams' of this song [Rudel 1978: 54]) the poet falls in love with the countess of Tripoli after hearing pilgrims speak of her: in order to see her he takes up the cross of pilgrimage and sets sail ('se croset et mes se en mar', [ibid.: 58]). In this fictionalised biographical account, love is framed by two acts of pilgrimage, one a religious pilgrimage, which incidentally carries the stories of the countess to Rudel, and the other an amorous pilgrimage which cloaks itself as a religious journey.

Rudel is one of the earliest poets to use religious pilgrimage as a metaphor for the emotional and/or physical journey towards amorous fulfilment. The metaphor is subsequently embraced by Petrarch, Dante, Shakespeare, and the Elizabethan poet Sir Philip Sidney (1554–86) in his romance *Arcadia*, which exists in three early versions. The earliest, manuscript text, written by 1581, is known as the *Old Arcadia*, to distinguish it from the revised, incomplete version printed posthumously in 1590 and now called the *New Arcadia*. In 1593, a hybrid text titled *The Countess of Pembroke's Arcadia* was published by Sidney's sister Mary, the Countess of Pembroke; it allied the revised *New Arcadia* with an adapted ending of the original *Old Arcadia* (Robertson 1973: xv–xix; Skretkowicz 1987: xiii–xiv). In Sidney's original conception, the *Arcadia* was a pastoral romance of five 'acts' (that is, books), punctuated by eclogues, which related the story of Basilius, Duke of Arcadia, who abandons the government of his country for a year in order to enter a pastoral retreat with his wife Gynecia and his daughters Pamela and Philoclea. Knowledge of the princesses' beauty comes to the princes Musidorus and Pyrocles and they adopt disguises as the shepherd Dorus and the Amazon Cleophila respectively, in order to gain access to the princesses, who have become the objects of their passion. The revised version of the *Arcadia* retains the narrative premise of Basilius's retreat and the princes' disguises, but it recasts the whole in an epic and Christianised format, adding digressions concerning the princes' heroic exploits in Asia Minor, bestowing a regal and stoic dignity on Pamela, and supplying the episode in which the queen Cecropia imprisons the princesses in an attempt to marry one of them to her son Amphialus, and thereby gain control of Arcadia. The castle in which the princesses are held is besieged by Basilius' allies, in a recasting of the Trojan legend: as John Carey has noted, the Cecropia episode in the *New Arcadia* recalls the *Iliad* in its depiction of 'the horror and beauty of war and warriors' (Carey 1987: 252). In this move to epic, the private places of the *Old Arcadia* are exchanged for the public battlefield, and love is transformed from an individual pilgrimage to an epic quest that is even more concerned with the securing of a country's political destiny than it is with individual desire. One may detect in these changes evidence of Sidney's 'deepening commitment to the intellectual French brand of Protestantism' current in the household of his father-in-law Francis Walsingham, as well as a personal desire for enhanced political significance and opportunity (Duncan-Jones 1991: 251). As a consequence of Sidney's revisions, the depiction of the princes as pilgrims for love, the inheritors of a dignified medieval tradition of *amor de lonh*, gives way to a world in which amorous union and political security are attained by the violent and laboursome travel of the epic quest; the incomplete state of the *New Arcadia* also means that in this particular text there is no end to the amorous and heroic labours of the princes.

This shift in the conceptualisation of travel between the *Old* and *New* versions of the *Arcadia* echoes the historical process identified by Jas' Elsner and Joan-Pau Rubiés in their introduction to *Voyages & Visions: Towards a Cultural History of Travel*. Elsner and Rubiés describe the cultural history of travel as 'a dialectic of dominant paradigms between two poles', which they identify as 'the transcendental vision of pilgrimage' and 'the open-ended process which typically characterizes modernity'. The former, they argue, prioritises the attainment of a goal and the consequent sense of (spiritual) fulfilment, whereas the latter defers fulfilment and elevates the act of travel above that of attainment (Elsner and Rubiés 1999: 5). Sidney's move from pastoral to epic can be read in the same light: I will argue in this essay that the hope for fulfilment which is intrinsic to *amor de lonh* and passionate pilgrimage is replaced in the *New Arcadia* by a concentration on the process or journey of love itself, a process which is laboursome, violent, dangerous, and subject to failure. Whereas in the pilgrimage model all emotional and physical energy is directed towards the hope of attaining the sacral site of the beloved, in the 'open-ended' process which concentrates on the journey itself there is no guarantee that this site can be reached. In the context of the history of travel, Elsner and Rubiés describe this resignation of the pilgrimage model of travel as a 'disenchantment' which signals the birth of the modern (1999: 45); in many ways the *New Arcadia* could be described as experiencing a similar disenchantment in the realm of love. Passion in the *New Arcadia* is as likely to constitute hatred, grief or anger (*OED*, 'passion', *n.*, 6a) as it is amorous feeling (*OED*, 8a), and even love itself seems to lead inexorably to death and loss rather than sexual and spiritual fulfilment.

*

The *Old Arcadia* opens with an account of a pilgrimage, the significance of which has been much debated in the context of the romance as a whole. Arcadia is a peaceful country until Basilius decides that he 'would needs undertake a journey to Delphos, there by the oracle to inform himself whether the rest of his life should be continued in like tenor of happiness as thitherunto it had been' (Robertson 1973: 5).[1] The oracle warns Basilius of princely thefts, 'uncouth love' and 'adultery' committed between himself and his wife. The reason for this sudden urge to undertake a religious journey is given tersely by the narrator: Basilius is 'not so much stirred with the care for his country and children as with the vanity which possesseth many who, making a perpetual mansion of this poor baiting place of man's life, are desirous to know the certainty of things to come, wherein there is nothing so certain as our continual uncertainty' (*Old*: 5). This comment brings Basilius's actual pilgrimage to Delphos into comparison with another kind of pilgrimage, the allegorical pilgrimage of life: a 'baiting place' (*OED*, 'bait', *v.*, sense 7) is a stopping place for the purpose of refreshment and changing horses on a journey. Within the terms and the setting of the romance itself, a visit to Delphos is not necessarily a culpable act: pilgrimages are a staple feature of the Greek romances, such as Heliodorus' *Aethiopica*, which were among Sidney's sources for the *Arcadia*. Elliptical and misunderstood oracles are likewise a common feature of these tales (one thinks, for example, of the riddling prophecy given to Thyamis by Isis in the *Aethiopica*: 'this maiden I deliver to you; you shall have her and not have her; you shall do wrong and slay her, but she shall not be slain' [Reardon 1989: 369]). On this occasion, however, the actual pilgrimage to Delphos is being brought into direct conflict with an allegorical understanding of pilgrimage and the Christian values that this allegory seeks to express and uphold. The oracle is described as an 'impiety' by the narrator, and Basilius' journey is taken as an indication of his misunderstanding of the 'real' journey of life: he possesses a worldly desire to know the 'certainty of things to come', and to fix his state of worldly happiness, both of which are manifestations of his failure to appreciate either the mutability of life or the providence of God (even as a pagan he could be expected to conceive of both). The allegorical understanding of life as a *peregrinatio* takes its ultimate spiritual inspiration from the catalogue of the faithful patriarchs in Hebrews 11: 13–16 who were 'aliens and strangers on earth' and 'longing for a better country', that is, heaven. It became a commonplace in late antique and medieval Christian culture, and was still widespread in post-Reformation culture, being used also by Calvin in *Institutes* III.x (Chew 1962; Wenzel 1973; Hahn 1973: 115ff.; Howard 1980).

Sidney's familiarity with the allegory of the *peregrinatio vitae* is clearly apparent in the *Old Arcadia*. At the end of the romance, Pyrocles and Musidorus face execution for their part in the supposed death of Basilius. They debate together on the nature of the afterlife, and Musidorus offers consolation in the form of a song eschewing fear, because 'Our life is but a step in dusty way' (*Old*: 374). The theme is given full treatment in the second eclogues, in which the shepherd Histor recites a song he overheard from Plangus, a nobleman who is himself a traveller, searching for Pyrocles and Musidorus to enlist their help in rescuing his beloved, Erona, from captivity. Plangus' complaint begins thus:

> Alas, how long this pilgrimage doth last?
> > What greater ills have now the heav'ns in store
> > To couple coming harms with sorrows past?
> Long since my voice is hoarse, and throat is sore,
> > With cries to skies, and curses to the ground;
> > But more I plain, I feel my woes the more.
> Ah where was first that cruel cunning found
> > To frame of earth a vessel of the mind,
> > Where it should be to self-destruction bound?
> What needed so high sprites such mansions blind?
> > Or wrapped in flesh what do they here obtain,
> > But glorious name of wretched human-kind?
> Balls to the stars, and thralls to Fortune's reign;
> > Turned from themselves, infected with their cage,
> > Where death is feared, and life is held with pain (*Old*: 147).

As can be seen here, the idea of life as a journey may express earthly despair just as easily as it may convey confidence in the heavenly country to which one is travelling. Such lamenting uses of *peregrinatio* draw on the wider sense of pilgrimage as a wandering journey, without an explicit destination; in this usage there are often shades of the exilic narratives of the books of Genesis and Exodus. A 'pilgrimage' in both medieval and Renaissance English could mean a journey (peregrination) or a sojourning (amongst strangers) (*OED*, 'pilgrimage', *n.*, 1a and 1b). Whilst both definitions may lend themselves to specifically Christian allegorisation, the latter fuses easily – as in this poem – with the Platonic theory of the body as a temporary abode, even prison, to the sojourning soul (*Phaedo*, 67–68; for Renaissance neoplatonism see Harrison 1903; Nelson 1958).

Such was the popularity of the allegorical *peregrinatio* that there is no need to search for an individual text that might have informed Sidney's use of it. However, it is worth noting that studies of Spenser's *The Faerie Queene* (1590 and 1596) have suggested possible links between that poem and known allegorical pilgrimage narratives. The first of these is Guillaume Deguileville's *Pilgrimage of the Life of Man*, written in two versions in 1330 and 1335 and widely copied and translated throughout the fourteenth, fifteenth and sixteenth centuries. This text was proposed as a Spenserian source by Padelford in 1931, and received extended attention in Rosamund Tuve's influential study *Allegorical Imagery* in 1966. There was, however, no printed English translation of Deguileville: those who hold that the influence of this pilgrimage text continued into the Renaissance tend to fall back on Lydgate's translation (1426) – although there is no proof that Spenser or Sidney had knowledge of it – and on the early seventeenth-century manuscript adaptation by Will Baspoole (Padelford 1931; Tuve 1966; see also Walls 1996 for a qualification of Tuve's continuity argument).

The second allegorical pilgrimage narrative to have been linked with *The Faerie Queene* is Stephen Bateman's *The Travayled Pylgrime* of 1569 (Koller 1942; Prescott 1989). This is a more persuasive proposition as a text that might have been known to Spenser and, possibly, Sidney. Most importantly, Bateman was a Protestant poet whose addition of Elizabethan encomium to his source (a Spanish version of the 1483 allegory *Le Chevalier délibéré* by Oliver de la Marche) bears legitimate comparison with Spenser's own chivalric poem. According to Prescott, the strength of the case lies in 'Bateman's status as the only other published *Protestant* allegorist who described the journey of a knight from error to salvation while praising the Tudors and denouncing Rome' (Prescott 1989: 194). As in the case of Deguileville, direct knowledge of Bateman's text in the Spenser-Sidney circle is impossible to prove, but its existence does indicate the continued use of the allegorical *peregrinatio* within the work of a self-consciously, even militantly, Protestant English poet. Two primary features of 'Protestant poetics' as identified by Barbara Kiefer Lewalski are the 'direct recourse to the Bible as a repository of truth' and the 'painstaking analysis of the personal religious life'; the pilgrim metaphor, with its biblical sanction in texts such as Hebrews 11: 13–16, and 1 Peter 2: 11, together with its opportunities for introspective analysis, is still a legitimate device in Protestant England, despite its associations with Catholic practice (Lewalski 1979: 4, 13, 93–94).

A Protestant poet would have looked as much to Calvin and Erasmus for his understanding of pilgrimage as to medieval allegories such as Deguileville's. Two of Erasmus's colloquies, his *De votis temere susceptis* (1522) and *Peregrinatio religionis ergo* (1526), provide an interesting gloss upon the pilgrimage undertaken by Basilius at the beginning of the *Arcadia*. Having received the oracle, Basilius attempts to deflect the events foretold in it, which are the theft of his elder daughter, the 'uncouth love' of his younger daughter, adultery between himself and his wife, and the occupation of his throne by a foreign power. His solution is to remove his family to their pastoral retreat, a move which is criticised openly by Philanax, who is given control of the state:

> I would ... have said the heavenly powers to be reverenced and not searched into, and their mercy rather by prayers to be sought than their hidden counsels by curiosity; these kinds of soothsaying sorceries (since the heavens have left us in ourselves sufficient guides) to be nothing but fancies wherein there must either be vanity or infallibleness, and so either not to be respected or not to be prevented. (*Old*: 7)

This speech is reminiscent of the criticisms levelled against contemporary pilgrimage by Erasmus in his colloquies. The speakers of the *Peregrinatio religionis ergo* are Ogygius, who has been on pilgrimage to Compostela, and Menedemus, the sceptic. Ogygius' description of the marvels he has seen is dismissed by Menedemus – 'I'm afraid many such affairs are contrived for profit' (Erasmus 1997b: 632). In *De votis temere susceptis*, Cornelius makes a similar observation about the antique monuments of Jerusalem, 'all of which I thought faked and contrived for the purpose of enticing naïve and credulous folk' (Erasmus 1997a: 37). Pilgrims are particularly vulnerable to the lure of curiosity: Menedemus assumes that Ogydius travelled 'out of curiosity, I dare say', to which the riposte is, 'On the contrary, out of devotion' (Erasmus 1997b: 623; on curiosity see also Zacher 1976 and Williams 1998: 23–24). The colloquy ends by contrasting the peregrination of the pilgrim with the domestic peregrinations of Menedemus:

> Here's how I wander about at home. I go into the living room and see that my daughters' chastity is safe. Coming out of there into my shop, I watch what my servants, male and female, are doing then to the kitchen, to see if any instruction is needed. From here to one place and another, observing what my children and my wife are doing, careful that everything be in order. (Erasmus 1997b: 650)

This passage is strikingly relevant to the operation of domestic government in the *Arcadia*. It has often been noted that Basilius's domestic arrangements are comically ill-conceived, and in recent political readings of the romance Basilius's misgovernment of the family emerges as a paradigm for the broader political failings of Arcadia (McCoy 1979; Worden 1996). The familial dangers held in check by Menedemus's domestic peregrinations all take place in the *Old Arcadia*: the chastity of Basilius's daughters is privately and then openly brought under attack from the princes when Musidorus elopes with Pamela and Pyrocles is discovered in Philoclea's bed; there is ample need for reproof in the servant household of Dametas, Miso and Mopsa; and Gynecia falls in love with Pyrocles.

Calvin provides another Renaissance context for reading Philanax's outburst. His tract on relics was translated into English as *A very profitable treatise* in 1561, and *Institutes* I.iv warns against the curiosity of the superstitious: this is a detail within a broader argument putting the case that 'mingled vanity and pride' lead men to 'vain speculation' about God rather than 'solid inquiry' (*Institutes* I.iv; see also Dana 1987: 90).

This exchange between Basilius and Philanax is an example of the 'superficial discrepancy', as C.S. Lewis calls it, between pagan practice and anachronistic Christian sentiment in Renaissance texts. Such discrepancies are common; Lewis makes this observation whilst discussing *The Winter's Tale*, in which Leontes receives an oracle from Delphos, yet Polixenes 'knows all about original sin' (Lewis 1954: 342). In the view of Erasmus and Calvin – and Philanax – pilgrimage and other curious or superstitious undertakings are vain and delusory enterprises which imperil godly domesticity.

The *Arcadia* is full of travellers, sojourners and displaced persons. Basilius's retreat to 'a solitary place' (*Old*: 6) turns his family into *peregrini* within their own country; Plangus, the singer of the lament discussed above, is in voluntary, wandering exile from his own country as he searches for the princes, and the princes themselves are travellers. Their journey begins as a straightforward sea voyage from Thessalia to Macedon, but a storm casts them up on the coast of Lydia, from where they travel through Asia, Syria and Egypt before arriving in Arcadia. The events of this journey are not recited in the *Old Arcadia*, but form part of the text's expansion in the revised version: Josephine Roberts has argued that this heroic journey (which she only fleetingly contrasts with the passionate pilgrimage of the *Old Arcadia*) is a mechanism by which the princes are educated in the 'architectonic' (comprehensive or sovereign) knowledge – in Sidney's understanding of the term, self-knowledge – necessary to their princely characters (Roberts 1978: 59, 274–75). Even Pyrocles' love for Philoclea is conceived on the move, when the princes see her picture whilst walking in their host's gallery in Mantinea (*Old*: 11), and the first desire provoked in Pyrocles is 'secretly to draw his dear friend a-walking to the desert of the two lodges' (*Old:* 12). Pyrocles even has difficulty at first in distinguishing between the desires of the lover and the traveller: 'Yet did not the poor youth at first know his disease, thinking it only such a kind of desire as he was wont to have to see unwonted sights' (*Old:* 12). It is whilst walking towards the lodges that Musidorus challenges Pyrocles' sudden desire for solitariness, and thereby learns that his friend is in love and has exchanged one kind of travelling for another – namely, a pilgrimage directed towards the attainment of his desire by means of entering the secluded lodges in disguise. Thus Pyrocles begins his journey towards the shrine of Philoclea's bed (attained at the end of book 3); this kind of pilgrimage is designated the *peregrinatio amoris* by Juergen Hahn (1973: 98). It is not long before Musidorus himself falls in love with Pamela. Once again, movement is the immediate consequence, as 'not being able to bear the vehement pain, he ran away through the grove, like a madman, hoping perchance (as the fever-sick folks do) that the change of places might ease his grief' (*Old:* 41). Here, the traditions of flight from passion (from the *Metamorphoses*) and love as madness (from the medieval romances of Tristan and Lancelot) fuse with the underlying metaphor of love as a form of travel.

Once Musidorus and Pyrocles are both lovers, their common purpose – which was threatened whilst Musidorus scorned passion – is reasserted, as is their common journey, their 'tragical pilgrimage' (*Old:* 43). The pilgrim metaphor captures both the singularity and the mutuality of the princes in love: their complaints work 'mutually' in one another to produce common woe – and common utterance – that still permits for the singularity of their individual passions. The passionate pilgrim, like the actual pilgrim, is cut adrift from his original community and isolated in thought and emotion, but at the same time he is brought into community with other pilgrims heading towards the same sacral site and speaking the same language of devotion. The primary expression of the pilgrim bond lies in the telling of stories within the pilgrim group. This tradition of the pilgrim tale goes back to Luke 24 and the two pilgrims on the road to Emmaus, who are discussing the events of the crucifixion when they are joined by Jesus who, in exchange for their account of recent events, explains to them 'what was said in the Scriptures concerning himself' (Luke 24: 27). The 'Emmaus paradigm' as it has been termed (Holloway 1985: 106) strictly requires the meeting of one pilgrim with two others, and the exchange of stories, but in a more dilute form it can be seen in the widespread association of pilgrims, and itinerancy in general, with the telling of tales. The princes, as strangers in the land of Arcadia, are called upon to tell their stories to nonpilgrims as well as to one another, and certain elements of these tales conform to the stereotype of the pilgrim narrative in being fabulations. Erasmus mocks pilgrim tales in the person of Cornelius, for whom the major benefit of his pilgrimage has been that 'whenever I like I'll have the vast pleasure of impressing both myself and others at gatherings or parties by telling lies about my travels' (Erasmus 1997a: 38). The princes' tales are not uniformly lies, but they are certainly not entirely trustworthy narratives: motivations, events and names are jumbled and rewritten in order to support and explain the princes' new identities, and to conceal their real reasons for being in Arcadia. (The princes' multiple identites are complicated yet further at the end of the *Old Arcadia* and the beginning of the *New* by their adoption of pseudonyms: they call themselves Palladius and Timopyrus in book 4 of the *Old Arcadia* and Palladius and Daiphantus in book 1 of the *New*).

At the beginning of book 3 of the *Old Arcadia*, Musidorus and Pyrocles return to the place where Pyrocles's passion was first revealed, and where their mutuality as fellow-travellers was momentarily challenged whilst Musidorus scorned love. On this second occasion, the location is the setting for an exchange of tales which confirms their common purposes:

they recounted one to another their strange pilgrimage of passions, omitting nothing which the open-hearted friendship is wont to lay forth, where there is cause to communicate both joys and sorrows – for, indeed, there is no sweeter taste of friendship than the coupling of their souls in this mutuality either of condoling or comforting, where the oppressed mind finds itself not altogether miserable, since it is sure of one which is feelingly sorry for his misery; and the joyful spends not his joy either alone or there where it may be envied, but may freely send it to such a well-grounded object, from whence he shall be sure to receive a sweet reflection of the same joy, and (as in a clear mirror of sincere goodwill) see a lively picture of his own gladness. Then would there arise betwixt them loving debates of their ladies' beauties, of their own constancies; and sometimes gloriously strive whether had been the most wretched. (*Old*: 168)

The competitive loquacity of pilgrims is a literary commonplace. Erasmus, for example, concludes *De votis temere susceptis* with Arnold's and Cornelius's plans for an evening of convivial drinking with friends, to see who can tell of the greatest marvels. The princes' story-telling also models the Renaissance ideal of friendship, based on Cicero's *De Amicitia*, which expounds such mutuality and mirroring. Friendship, according to Laelius in *De Amicitia*, may be defined as 'a complete identity of feeling about all things in heaven and earth' (Cicero 1971: 187). He continues, 'when a man thinks of a true friend, he is looking at himself in the mirror' (Cicero 1971: 189). Friends share a common purpose and identity, and so 'will compete with one another in the noblest way' – especially in matters of love (Cicero 1971: 194). The recitation of their individual 'pilgrimage of passions' therefore binds the princes together more closely as pilgrims in a common cause and as friends in the Ciceronian model. It also brings them into competition as they enter into 'loving debates', lauding their ladies and celebrating their own travails – just as the friends of *De Amicitia* become competitors and Erasmus's pilgrims compete in their telling of marvels.

The princes' intention in setting out on their original journey is to 'exercise their virtues and increase their experience' (*Old:* 11), which is the standard justification for travel, as expressed in Jerome Turler's treatise, *De peregrinatione*, translated into English as *The Traveiler* in 1575:

> For since Experience is the greatest part of human wisdome, and the same is increased by traveil: I suppose there is no man will deney, but that a man may become the wiser by traveiling. (1575: sig.A3r)

As Blair Worden has noted, the travels of the princes, similar to those undertaken by Sidney himself, are appropriate for young men who are being educated for a public and military role: the princes, like Sidney, are careful to note the military strength of the countries they visit (Worden 1996: 297–98; these activities also correspond to the advice given in Turler 1575: E4v). Yet Musidorus is more than just a traveller: he is a teller of travellers' tales, and he is aware of the nuances associated with different types of actual and metaphorical travel. For example, he contrasts his own physical and emotional travels in a story told to Pamela in which the prince who set out to learn 'experience by travel' (*Old:* 104) found himself taking on the guise of a shepherd and then becoming trapped in 'a maze of longing'. As Howard (1980: 7–8) points out, pilgrimages and labyrinths are often connected with one another: for example, mazes could be used in medieval times as a pilgrimage in miniature, with the pilgrim proceeding on his knees to the centre point.

Musidorus is presenting himself as a 'real' traveller turned metaphorical pilgrim. Thus Musidorus's traveller's tale is used as a revelatory mechanism: it is through this story – the disguised tale of a traveller's disguise – that Pamela 'did immediately catch hold of his signifying himself to be a prince'. In this case, the proverbial wisdom that 'A Traveller may lie with authority' (Tilley 1950: T476) is turned on its head, and the traveller's tale reveals the truth. So powerful is this traveller's tale that Sidney makes a comparison with music, which was regarded as the supreme mechanism for moving the passions (Reiss 1999: 512):

> She found he meant the tale by himself, and that he did under that covert manner make her know the great nobleness of his birth. But no music could with righter accords possess her senses than every passion he expressed had his mutual working in her. (*Old*: 106)

In Castiglione's *Book of the Courtier,* Count Lodovico reminds the company that 'the heavens make harmony as they move, and that as our own souls are formed on the same principle they are awakened and have their faculties, as it were, brought to life through music' (Castiglione 1967: 94–95). Music is used in sacred places to praise God, by labourers to stir them to work and to relieve tedium, and by mariners to calm themselves after storms. Finally, 'weary pilgrims find solace in music on their long and exhausting journey, as so often do chained and fettered prisoners in their misery' (Castiglione 1967: 96). So, to complete his assault on Pamela's passions, Musidorus sings a song. 'The music added to the tale', Pamela weakens, and Musidorus reveals he intends another journey, namely their flight from the 'unworthy bondage' suffered by the princesses under Dametas's charge.

Yet not all Musidorus's tales are such trustworthy signifiers. In order to effect his escape with Pamela, Musidorus designs a 'far-fet tale' to trick Mopsa, and this tale is also about a travelling shepherd. He invents a story about Apollo, exiled from heaven and living as Admetus's herdsman, who, 'wearied with travel' (*Old*: 194), arrives in that very spot and rests by a tree, where, because of his lamenting, he is pardoned by Jupiter and received again as a god. By telling Mopsa that Apollo has given the tree the quality of granting the wishes of whoever sits in it, Musidorus ensures that she waits in the tree whilst he and Pamela make their escape. Mopsa is even symbolically 'muffled' about the face, becoming an emblem of the delusion and blindness attendant upon believing disguised tales told by the disguised. When the princes are brought to trial, the evidence of their multiple disguises sends Philanax into a paroxysm of rage as he outlines Pyrocles's crimes:

> This man, whom to begin withal I know not how to name, since being come into this country unaccompanied like a lost pilgrim, from a man grew a woman, from a woman a ravisher of women, thence a prisoner, and now a prince. (*Old*: 387)

As well as being notorious tale-tellers, pilgrims are also poets of praise, uttering hymns of joy when they reach their destination (Howard 1980: 43). The end point of Pyrocles' passionate pilgrimage is Philoclea's chamber: as he approaches he is compared to Aeneas (*Old*: 232) – the archetypal traveller – and when he finally holds Philoclea in his arms, to lay her on her bed, he recalls the shepherd Philisides' song, 'What tongue can her perfections tell?' (*Old*: 238–42). The beginning of the song is heavy with Petrarchan detail: the beloved's hair is made from 'fine threads of finest gold', her forehead is whiter than snow, her eyes black stars, her ears a lover's maze. These idealised traits gradually give way, however, to an Ovidian hymn of love, a blazon which is used to map and explore the beauties of Philoclea's body. The spiritual path of love which led Pyrocles to the chamber is superseded by the physical 'way' which leads between Philoclea's breasts to the 'joyous field' of her waist. Pyrocles' eyes are now travellers too: 'the wandering thought' might be distracted by her sides, were it not for the fact that 'Her belly there glad sight doth fill'. His eyes encounter her thighs like a sailor approaching land: they exceed 'Albion cliffs' in their smooth whiteness. The veins in her hand are 'sapphire-coloured brooks' which 'sweet islands make in that sweet land'. The geography of the female body is celebrated by the traveller until the end of the poem, when Petrarchan and Neoplatonic conventions reassert themselves in the language of devotion. The coloniser's voice gives way once again to that of the Neoplatonic love-pilgrim, who contemplates the inner virtue shrined within outer beauty:

Thus hath each part his beauty's part;
But how the Graces do impart
To all her limbs a special grace,
Becoming every time and place,
Which doth e'en beauty beautify,
And most bewitch the wretched eye!
How all this is but a fair inn
Of fairer guest which dwells within,
Of whose high praise, and praiseful bliss,
Goodness the pen, heav'n paper is;
The ink immortal fame doth lend.
As I begun, so must I end:
   No tongue can her perfections tell,
   In whose each part all pens may dwell. (*Old*: 242)

In the version of this scene printed in the 1593 composite *Arcadia* Pyrocles is not granted the sight of Philoclea's body as he lays her on her bed and so there is no hymn of praise. Instead, he lies down beside her and they fall asleep. There is no sense of a journey over, no allusion to the path of love mapped on Philoclea's body, and no Ovidian challenge to the language of Neoplatonic love. In their 'chaste embracements' the lovers present a picture of 'how gladly (if death came) their souls would go together' (Evans 1977: 690).

The fact that the journey of love in the composite *Arcadia* is unconsummated highlights the change in the way in which metaphors of travel are used in the *New Arcadia* and in the adapted ending of the *Old Arcadia* which was published with the revised romance in the composite version of 1593. The shepherd Philisides (a figure for the author) provides the key to this: in the *Old Arcadia* he undertakes 'perpetual absence' when spurned by his beloved, Mira (*Old*: 341), and it is this sense of the lover-as-absent which dominates the revised *Arcadia*. Being absent is quite different from being a pilgrim: it is a negative identity, a forced or motivated withdrawal from amorous action. Another shadowy figure also removes her presence in the fourth book: the shepherdess Urania, plagued by the amorous persistence of the shepherds Strephon and Claius, leaves the country 'upon a strange occasion, giving withal strait commandment to these two by writing that they should tarry in Arcadia until they heard from her' (*Old*: 328). The importance of this moment for the *New Arcadia*[2] becomes immediately clear at the beginning of book 1, which opens with Strephon and Claius's lamenting recollection of Urania's embarkation:

> But (woe is me) yonder, yonder did she put her foot into the boat, at that instant, as it were, dividing her heavenly beauty between the earth and the sea. But when she was embarked did you not mark how the winds whistled and the seas danced for joy, how the sails did swell with pride, and all because they had Urania? (*New*: 4)

Katherine Duncan-Jones, reading Urania as 'Heavenly Beauty, Venus Urania', argues that her departure at the beginning of the *New Arcadia* sets the tone for the whole of the revised version of the romance: heavenly beauty has gone, 'and only her earthly counterpart, Venus Pandemos, remains in Arcadia' (1966: 129).

Hot on the heels of a story of absence comes a story of displacement and loss: the shepherds' laments are interrupted by the sight of the shipwrecked Musidorus, who almost casts himself back into the sea when he realises he has lost Pyrocles. The opening of the revised Arcadia borrows from the beginning of the *Aethiopica*, in which the lovers Theagenes and Charikleia – displaced from their home because of their love – are discovered shipwrecked on a beach. In the *New Arcadia*, displacement and disappearance, rather than pilgrimage, are the natural consequences of love. When Pyrocles falls in love with Philoclea he disappears, leaving Musidorus to complain of his loss:

> What have I deserved of thee to be thus banished of thy counsels? Heretofore I have accused the sea, condemned the pirates, and hated my evil fortune that deprived me of thee; but now thyself is the sea which drowns my comfort; thyself is the pirate that robs thyself from me; thy own will becomes my evil fortune. (*New*: 55)

Throughout the whole of the *New Arcadia* there also roams the figure of Helen of Corinth, whose love for Amphialus has made her an itinerant:

For this cause have I left my country, putting in hazard how my people will in time deal by me, adventuring what perils or dishonours might ensue, only to follow him who proclaimeth hate against me, and to bring my neck unto him, if that may redeem my trespass and assuage his fury. (*New*: 65)

Helen's pursuit of Amphialus has left one separation behind her, in Corinth, and is directed towards another separation, of life from body. For Helen, finding Amphialus will not lead to worship at the shrine of the beloved, or physical consummation, or the centre of the maze of longing, but a reparation for an earlier loss. (Amphialus's hatred towards her is caused by the fact that Helen was loved by his friend, Philoxenus, who attacked Amphialus and was killed in self-defence.)

Whereas the first three books of the *Old Arcadia* move towards the desired union of the lovers, books 4 and 5 anticipate the losses, absences, estrangements and deaths of the revised version: the marriage bonds of Gynecia and Basilius appear to be shattered by death, the lovers are torn apart, and the princes are violently separated from their pastoral *alter egos* of Dorus and Cleophila. Public as well as personal woes are caused by absence: Basilius's absence from government is seen as precipitating 'the pangs of uttermost peril' experienced by Arcadia when the Duke's quixotic exile seems to have been transformed into the permanent estrangement of death (*Old*: 351). According to the fourth eclogues, the country is left 'wandr'ing from all good direction' (*Old:* 349) and even Philanax enters a state of abstraction that is 'like a man gone a far journey from himself' (*Old:* 359). In the *New Arcadia* Plangus's story is a tragedy arising from a catalogue of absences: his 'many times leaving of the court' (*New*: 216) to visit his mistress during her husband's absences leads his father to discover and desire the woman himself. Plangus is sent away on military duties, his mistress forgets this 'absent Plangus' and marries his father (*New*: 217). Her hostility to Plangus results in his voluntary exile and eventually leads to his exclusion from the succession, because his enemies and his absence have worked together to diminish 'the wavering people's affection' (*New:* 222).

Whereas in the *Old Arcadia* the lovers' thoughts are directed towards the attainment of the object of their desires, in the *New*

Arcadia a sense of present loss, rather than future attainment, dominates the language of love. The identity taken on by Pyrocles is not that of Cleophila but of Zelmane, an Amazon who loved him but is now dead (*New*: 268). The original Zelmane dies with the language of loss on her lips – seeing Pyrocles's tears she cries 'How largely am I recompensed for my losses!' (*New:* 267) – and the Zelmane who has been lost to death casts a shadow of loss over the love affair of Pyrocles-Zelmane and Philoclea in the *New Arcadia*. Loss seems to have asserted once again its power over love when the wicked queen Cecropia stages Philoclea's execution: Zelmane is watching and gives vent to her anguish in the language of separation:

> Alas, why should they divide such a head from such a body? ... She is gone! and gone with her all my hope, all my wishing ... . O cruel divorce of the sweetest marriage that ever was in nature! Philoclea is dead – and dead is with her all goodness, all sweetness, all excellency! (*New:* 433)

Passion is not a pilgrimage for Pyrocles-Zelmane, as it had been for Pyrocles-Cleophila: the 'wandering muse' into which Zelmane sinks following the supposed execution of Philoclea presents only 'vexations' to his mind rather than the vision of desire attained. The 'wandering' of his thoughts provides no inspiration for possible action, only perpetual weeping, which in romance is a symbol of emotional and physical paralysis (*New:* 433). The associations of travel in the revised romance therefore lie with blind and directionless wandering rather than with the longed-for attainment of a sacred space, as was true of the *Old Arcadia*.

Kidnapping and captivity, rather than elected travel, characterise the patterns of travel and movement in the *New Arcadia*. Love is not a pilgrimage, but a form of imprisonment: this idea is heralded in the besieging of Erona, developed in the tale of the princes' imprisonment at the hands of Andromana and fulfilled when the princesses and Zelmane are kidnapped and imprisoned by Cecropia, who desires the Arcadian throne for her son Amphialus. Metaphorical immurements also take over from passionate pilgrimages and Zelmane describes his disguise – originally adopted to facilitate his pilgrimage – as a form of captivity:

Alas, who ever but I was imprisoned in liberty, and banished, being still present? To whom but me have lovers been jailers, and honour a captivity? (*New:* 224)

The release of the princesses can be achieved only by single combat, and the pseudonyms of the knights who fight on their behalf are revelatory: they present themselves not in the traditional anonymous guise of unknown lover, or loving shepherd, but as the 'Forsaken Knight' (Musidorus; *New:* 405) and the 'Knight of the Tomb' (Parthenia in disguise; *New:* 396). Parthenia's armour becomes her tomb as she dies, thus underlining the fact that in this version of the story love is associated with loss, the absence and estrangement of death, and the cessation of action. Even the intercourse of friendship is now a 'bartering of miseries' rather than a mutual exchange of stories (*New:* 127).

The interplay of passionate, private narratives and political, public narratives in the original and revised *Arcadia*s has long been a subject of critical debate. Early commentators, such as Gabriel Harvey, in *Pierces Supererogation* (1593), read the composite 1593 *Arcadia* as a compendious text, notable for 'amorous Courting' as well as 'sage counselling' and 'valorous fighting' (Garrett 1996: 131). However, since Milton in *Eikonoklastes* (1649) castigated Charles I's use of Pamela's prayer and described the *Arcadia* as 'no serious Book' but a 'vain amatorious Poem' (Garrett 1996: 248), there has been persistent critical anxiety about the 'amatorious' nature of the text. Horace Walpole's attack in 1758 on what he regarded as Sidney's over-blown reputation, and his description of the *Arcadia* as a 'tedious, lamentable, pedantic, pastoral romance, which the patience of a young virgin in love cannot now wade through' (Garrett 1996: 286) continued to produce ripples of unease in twentieth-century criticism. Walter Davis countered this anti-amorous tradition by arguing that the *Arcadia* describes 'the perfection of the hero through love' (Davis 1965: 82) and A.C. Hamilton robustly allied the books of the *Old Arcadia* with different aspects of love: the 'catalogue of love's variety', 'the triumph of love', 'love-game comedy', 'love's consequences' and the 'judgement of love' (Hamilton 1977: 51–54). The most sustained defence of the amatory nature of the *Arcadia* was undertaken by Mark Rose, who expounded a theory of 'heroical love' (Rose 1968:12) in defence of this 'amatorious Poem'.

Sidney's use of the pilgrimage metaphor in the *Old Arcadia* in fact operates to unite the private and the public sides of the romance: the princes are young men learning 'experience by travel' before entering the political stage as rulers themselves, and they are also young men encountering the workings of love through the private and metaphorical pilgrimage of passion. Their mutual language of love-devotion binds them together more closely in a Ciceronian ideal of friendship, and their pilgrim tales at the same time enhance their amorous progress, as they reveal their true identities to the princesses. In the *New Arcadia*, however, love is figured not as a pilgrimage but as the precursor to endless wandering, kidnap, imprisonment, loss and absence. In this world of death and loss, it is not surprising to find that, near the end of Sidney's revision, he inserts another journey to Delphos. This journey takes place within the context of the princesses' imprisonment: faced with Anaxius's demand that he should be married to Pamela, Basilius 'was so perplexed that, not able to determine, he took the common course of men, to fly only then to devotion when they want resolution' (*New*: 457). This time the journey to Delphos is an act of devotion, not vanity, curiosity or superstition, and so it is Philanax who is sent to discern 'the counsel of Apollo'. The oracle speaks not in 'dark, wonted speeches, but plainly to be understood' and advises that the princesses are reserved for those 'better beloved of the gods'; it also declares that Philanax and Basilius will become 'fully agreed in the understanding of the former prophecy'. Soon after this, the *New Arcadia* breaks off, leaving the reader to wonder whether Sidney's plans for the later books of the *New Arcadia* would have redeemed the private pilgrimage of love as well. I suspect not, and would point to the story of Argalus and Parthenia in explanation. Their married love is the standard by which all the other amorous narratives of the *New Arcadia*, including those of the princes, are judged and found wanting; and their love is shown to be mutual and at rest, rather than individual and itinerant. Once married, Argalus and Parthenia are found at home together rather than roaming in search of one another. When the messenger from Basilius arrives with the request for Argalus's assistance, he finds a vision of domesticated heroism: Argalus is 'at a castle of his own, sitting in a parlour with the fair Parthenia, he reading in a book the stories of Hercules, she by him, as to hear him read' (*New*: 371). The days of their own labours and travels are over, and so it is with prophetic sorrow that Parthenia cries, 'And are you so soon resolved to leave me?' (*New:* 372). Married love in the *New Arcadia* sets its face against travel, both actual and metaphorical, in favour of domestic peace and security: the tragedy of their story is that Argalus's departure leads inexorably to their common tomb rather than back to their shared home. Whereas in the *Old Arcadia* the pilgrimage of passion offers the hope of union and a cure for the pains of *amor de lonh*, travel in the *New Arcadia* figures restlessness, loss, absence and separation. In abandoning the hope of fulfilment and union offered by the pilgrimage model, Sidney's revised *Arcadia* thereby partakes of the 'disenchantment' which separates the medieval conception of travel from that of modernity.

Notes

1 Robertson (1973) will subsequently be referred to as *Old*, followed by the page number.
2 Stretkowicz (1987) will be referred to as *New*, followed by the page number.

References

Carey, J. (1987) 'Structure and Rhetoric in *Arcadia*', in D. Kay (ed.) *Sir Philip Sidney: An Anthology of Modern Criticism*. Oxford: Clarendon Press.

Castiglione, B. (1967) *The Book of the Courtier*, trans. G. Bull. Harmondsworth: Penguin.

Chew, S.C. (1962) *The Pilgrimage of Life*. Port Washington, N.Y. and London: Kennikat Press.

Cicero (1971) *On the Good Life*, trans. M. Grant. Harmondsworth: Penguin.

Dana, M. (1987) 'The Providential Plot of the *Old Arcadia*', in D. Kay (ed.) *Sir Philip Sidney: An Anthology of Modern Criticism*. Oxford: Clarendon Press.

Davis, W. (1965) 'A Map of Arcadia: Sidney's Romance in its Tradition', in W.R. Davis and R.A. Lanham (eds.) *Sidney's Arcadia*. New Haven, C.T. and London: Yale University Press.

Duncan-Jones, K. (1966) 'Sidney's Urania', *Review of English Studies* 17: 123–32.

—— (1991) *Sir Philip Sidney: Courtier Poet*. London: Hamish Hamilton.

Elsner, J. and Rubiés, J.-P. (1999) *Voyages & Visions: Towards a Cultural History of Travel*. London: Reaktion Books.

Erasmus (1997a) *Collected Works of Erasmus volume 39: Colloquies*, trans. C.R. Thompson. Toronto, Buffalo and London: University of Toronto Press.

———— (1997b) *Collected Works of Erasmus volume 40: Colloquies*, trans. C.R. Thompson. Toronto, Buffalo and London: University of Toronto Press.

Evans, M. (1977) (ed.) *The Countess of Pembroke's Arcadia*. Harmondsworth: Penguin.

Garrett, M. (1996) *Sidney: The Critical Heritage*. London and New York: Routledge.

Hahn, J. (1973) *The Origins of the Baroque Concept of Peregrinatio*. Chapel Hill: University of North Carolina Press.

Hamilton, A.C. (1977) *Sir Philip Sidney*. Cambridge: Cambridge University Press.

Harrison, J.S. (1903) *Platonism in English Poetry of the Sixteenth and Seventeenth Centuries*. New York: Columbia University Press.

Holloway, J.B. (1985) 'The Vita nuova: Paradigms of Pilgrimage', *Dante Studies* 103: 103–24

Howard, D. (1980) *Writers and Pilgrims: Medieval Pilgrimage Narratives and their Posterity*. Berkeley: University of California Press.

Koller, K. (1942) 'The Travayled Pylgrime by Stephen Batman and Book Two of *The Faerie Queene*', *Modern Language Quarterly* 3: 535–41.

Lewalski, B.K. (1979) *Protestant Poetics and the Seventeenth-Century Religious Lyric*. Princeton: Princeton University Press.

Lewis, C.S. (1954) *Poetry and Prose in the Sixteenth Century*. Oxford: Clarendon Press.

McCoy, R.C. (1979) *Sir Philip Sidney: Rebellion in Arcadia*. New Brunswick, N.J.: Rutgers University Press.

Nelson, J.C. (1958) *Renaisssance Theory of Love: The Context of Giordano Bruno's 'Eroici Furori'*. New York: Columbia.

Padelford, F.M. (1931) 'Spenser and *The Pilgrimage of the Life of Man*', *Studies in Philology* 28: 211–18.

Prescott, A.L. (1989) 'Spenser's Chivalric Restoration: From Bateman's *Travayled Pylgrime* to the Redcrosse Knight', *Studies in Philology* 86:166–97.

Reardon, B.P. (1989) *Collected Ancient Greek Novels*. Berkeley: University of California Press.

Reiss, T.J. (1999) 'Cartesian Aesthetics', in G.P.Norton (ed.) *The Cambridge History of Literary Criticism*, vol. III: The Renaissance. Cambridge: Cambridge University Press.

Roberts, J.A. (1978) *Architectonic Knowledge in the 'New Arcadia': Sidney's Use of the Heroic Journey*. Salzburg: Institut für Englische Sprache und Literatur.

Robertson, J. (1973) (ed.) *The Countess of Pembroke's Arcadia (The Old Arcadia)*. Oxford: Clarendon Press.

Rose, M. (1968) *Heroic Love: Studies in Sidney and Spenser*. Cambridge, M.A.: Harvard University Press.

Rudel, J. (1978) *The Songs of Jaufré Rudel*, ed. R.T. Pickens. Toronto: Pontifical Institute of Mediaeval Studies.

Skretkowicz, V. (1987) (ed.) *The Countess of Pembroke's Arcadia (The New Arcadia)*. Oxford: Clarendon Press, 1987.

Tilley, M.P. (1950) *A Dictionary of the Proverbs in England in the Sixteenth and Seventeenth Centuries: A Collection of Proverbs Found in English Literature and the Dictionaries of the Period*. Ann Arbor: University of Michigan Press.

Turler, J. (1575) *The Traveiler*, London: William How, for Abraham Veale.

Tuve, R. (1966) *Allegorical Imagery: Some Mediaeval Books and their Posterity*. Princeton: Princeton University Press.

Walls, K. (1996) 'Medieval "Allegorical Imagery" in c.1630: Will. Baspoole's revision of *The Pilgrimage of the Lyfe of the Manhode*', in M.J. Toswell and E.M. Tyler (eds),

Studies in English Language and Literature – 'Doubt wisely': Papers in honour of E.G. Stanley. London and New York: Routledge.

Wenzel, S. (1973) 'The Pilgrimage of Life as a Late Medieval Genre', *Mediaeval Studies* 35: 370–88.

Williams, W. (1998) *Pilgrimage and Narrative in the French Renaissance: 'The Undiscovered Country'.* Oxford: Clarendon Press.

Worden, B. (1996) *The Sound of Virtue: Philip Sidney's 'Arcadia' and Elizabethan Politics.* New Haven, C.T. and London: Yale University Press.

Zacher, C. (1976) *Curiosity and Pilgrimage: The Literature of Discovery in Fourteenth Century England.* Baltimore, M.D.: Johns Hopkins University Press.

Narratives of Transformation: Pilgrimage Patterns and Authorial Self-Presentation in Three Pilgrimage Texts

Alexia Petsalis-Diomidis
University College, Dublin

Introduction

This paper explores a theme important in pilgrimage narratives from a variety of cultures: the expression of the author/pilgrim's developing understanding of the meaning and significance of his or her pilgrimage. It does so through three case studies: readings of three first-person narratives from widely differing chronological, cultural and religious milieux. The first narrative is Aelius Aristides' *The Sacred Tales*, an ancient Greek text written AD *c.* 170, which evokes the culture of Graeco-Roman healing pilgrimage; the second is Friar Felix Fabri's *Evagatorium in Terrae Sanctae* ('Wanderings in the Holy Land'), a Latin narrative of Christian pilgrimage to the Holy Land written *c.*1484–8; and the third is Pierre Loti's *Un pèlerin d'Angkor* ('An Angkor Pilgrim'), a French text relating a personal (and initially nonreligious) pilgrimage to the temples of Angkor in what was then French Indo-China, published in 1912. These three narratives were produced in cultures with profoundly different traditions of pilgrimage, including its practice, its cultural meanings and the modes of its description. These significant differences immediately raise the question of the meaning and usefulness of attaching the label 'pilgrimage narratives' to all three texts, and invite a reasoning for the exercise of comparison across cultures and across time.

On the question of definition two issues need to be considered: whether these texts were written in and received as part of a tradition of pilgrimage writing in their own cultural contexts (a question of genre), and whether we, as twenty-first century cultural historians, can recognise the type of activity or process they are describing as 'pilgrimage' (a question of content). In this context, I use a broad definition of pilgrimage primarily as a journey undertaken for religious reasons, but also including nonreligious journeys motivated by a strong personal desire.[1] First let us consider Aristides' *The Sacred Tales*. In Graeco-Roman culture there was no distinct literary genre of pilgrimage writing, although we may choose to see periegetic travel writing, such as Pausanias's *Description of Greece*, and texts concerned with centres of pilgrimage, such as Lucian's *Alexander* and the *Syrian Goddess*, as modes of describing ancient pilgrimage. Aristides' text identifies itself by its title as a *hieros logos* ('sacred story') and thereby as part of a genre of narrating the mythological achievements of a god. He adapts this model by focusing exclusively on the god's achievements in relation to himself. In terms of content, Aristides writes about journeys undertaken at the command of the god (sacred journeys), and the goal of these pilgrimages (which are sometimes given the official term for pilgrimage, *theoria*) is bodily healing. The second text under consideration, Fabri's *Evagatorium in Terrae Sanctae*, is part of a well-established medieval tradition of descriptions of Christian pilgrimage to the Holy Land which stretched back to Late Antique accounts, such as that of Egeria. At the opening he expressly brings attention to the fact that he does not give the work the title of 'pilgrimage' (*peregrinatio*) but 'wandering' (*evagatorium*) (Fabri (1843–9) 2A) and explains that he includes information on geography and amusing anecdotes not strictly related to the sites in the Holy Land. Throughout the narrative, however, he does refer to his journey as a *peregrinatio*, he discusses at length its religious purpose and he warns against the dangers of *curiositas*.[2] In this way we can see Fabri positioned at the cusp between medieval pilgrimage culture and a nascent Renaissance humanism expressed in ethnographic travel writing. In the *Evagatorium*, Fabri describes his journeys and the landscape of the Holy Land and often he recalls his own feelings as a pilgrim. The third text, Loti's *Un pèlerin d'Angkor*, seems to push the definition of pilgrimage almost to breaking point: the journey described is not undertaken for religious reasons but for personal ones, and although the goal of the journey is a sacred complex it is not part of the religious tradition of the author.[3] Nevertheless, as we will see, the experience of this journey eventually offers Loti religious enlightenment. Moreover, through the title of the work and several references to contemporary Buddhist pilgrims to Angkor, Loti explicitly places himself within a pilgrimage discourse. The underlying paradigm, though, which developed during the European Enlightenment, is that of secular travel as exploration of unknown landscapes and cultures and eventually of the unknown self. It has been argued that this is a development of a pilgrimage tradition.[4] The prominence of the subjective self as opposed to an 'objective' discourse of travel is a particularly French (as opposed to Anglo-Saxon) feature and can be seen in the context of the fragmentation of discourses in the twentieth century. All three texts, then, were written within a tradition of pilgrimage writing in their own cultural context. They describe journeys of immense personal significance, driven by the pilgrims' desires (which are explicitly religious in the case of Aristides and Fabri), and these are activities that we can recognise as 'pilgrimages', albeit of very different kinds. Crucially, the journeys are identified by the authors as 'pilgrimages' in ancient Greek, Latin and French (*theoria*, *peregrinatio*, *pèlerinage*) and are presented within these particular cultural traditions of pilgrimage. We can, therefore, talk about these texts as 'pilgrimage narratives'.

Bearing in mind the cultural specificity of these three pilgrimage texts and the delicate nature of cross-cultural comparison, this paper will focus on a particular theme which is prominent in all three texts: the authors' expressions of a changing understanding of the meaning of their pilgrimage. There are two main reasons for undertaking this analysis. Firstly, as I will argue, this theme is fundamental in all three texts and is intimately linked to the authors' self-presentation (despite different models of self and personhood available in each culture). The examination of the similarities as well as the differences in the use of this theme can offer insights into the different kinds of pilgrimage and self-presentation that are being constructed. Secondly, the analysis of the literary renegotiation of the meaning of pilgrimage in three very different pilgrimage narratives opens the possibilities for refining our definitions of pilgrimage: it is suggested at the end that this theme is an important feature of the *practice* of pilgrimage. Although the basis for the comparison of these texts is purely aesthetic, it would also be possible to locate them in a historical continuum of European pilgrimage writing.

Before proceeding to examine the narratives individually it is important to clarify that the discussion is concerned with *texts* and authorial personae rather than the real experiences of the authors. Aristides, Fabri and Loti all made the journeys of pilgrimage on which their narratives are based, and it is entirely possible that the authors' experiences of pilgrimage involved a developing sense of the meaning of that experience (though this is, of course, wholly unverifiable). Nevertheless, the texts they produced are finished literary products written many years after the pilgrimages described.[5] Aristides and Fabri actually draw attention to the process of composition of their narratives. Aristides emphasises that he is unable to write about all the miracles granted to him by Asklepios and that he is selectively drawing together fragments of experience into a coherent narrative pattern (Aristides (1958) XLVII.1, XLVIII.1–4). Both Aristides and Fabri assert that their texts are based on records and diaries kept during the pilgrimage: on one level this bolsters the credibility of the stories and evokes a sense of recorded presence (Aristides (1958) XLVIII.2,3,8, XLIX.26,30, L.25 and Fabri (1843–9) 25A–B); but on another level, it points to the difference between these records of experience as they occurred and the published versions which were written as literary works with the benefit of leisure and hindsight.[6] Although the diaries referred to in *The Sacred Tales* and the *Evagatorium* may even have been invented for rhetorical effect, Loti is certainly known to have kept a *Journal intime* throughout his life, including the period of his pilgrimage to Angkor, though this diary is not mentioned in the narrative. Parts of the *Journal intime* were published posthumously, but the section covering the pilgrimage to Angkor was first published in 1989 and then only in a limited facsimile edition.[7] A comparison of the two texts reveals that Loti changed the story of his pilgrimage at various points, for instance adding a third full day of sightseeing at Angkor that never actually happened (Loti (1996): 64–72). All three texts, then, are polished literary creations which retrospectively impose narratives on the pilgrimage experiences of the past. Aristides and Loti could have chosen to expunge their original (mistaken) expectations of their pilgrimages; and Fabri could have chosen to omit his first pilgrimage to the Holy Land which was so disappointing that he felt the need to make a second, more satisfactory, journey. That they do not suggests that the feature of thwarted or mistaken expectation was one that each author consciously chose to include. How is the consequent theme of the renegotiation of the author's understanding of his pilgrimage used in the three texts?

Aelius Aristides, *The Sacred Tales*[8]

At the opening, Aristides defines his subject as 'the achievements of the Saviour' (XLVII.1). The epithet 'Saviour' was commonly used for Asklepios, the god of healing, and in particular it was used in the context of his cult at Pergamon in Asia Minor. Aristides further specifies the 'foreknowledge' of the god, and mentions several elements associated with the traditional healing cult of this god (XLVII.3): revelatory dreams; the 'storms' of his body; submitting to the god as to a doctor. The first episode, which is narrated in great detail (taking up almost the whole of Book One of the surviving six, numbered orations XLVII to LI), is the story of his stomach, its symptoms and the remedies recommended by Asklepios (XLVII.4–61). This initial focus on the author/pilgrim's body dramatises an initial understanding of the pilgrimage to Asklepios as a traditional search for bodily healing.

Only later, in Book Two, does Aristides recount the original circumstances and motivation for his pilgrimage to Asklepios (XLVIII.5–7, 60–70). As a talented and ambitious young orator from the province of Asia, he journeyed to Rome in order to declaim in the capital and advance his career. His illness, already incipient before he set out, is said to have become worse on the journey to Rome, and worse again on the return. Aristides' career is presented as being curtailed by his illness and his inability to travel. The doctors are unable to help him and in desperation suggest that he visit the warm springs near Smyrna. Here Asklepios made the first of his many revelations to Aristides and summoned him to Pergamon (XLVIII.7). The goal of the pilgrimage is thus presented as the restoration of bodily health in order to resume the practice of oratory, which involved declaiming and travelling.

The typical pattern of pilgrimage to Asklepios involved a journey to his sanctuary and there performing rituals of cleansing and sacrifice in preparation for sleeping in special buildings, in the hope of receiving a revelatory dream from the god. The cure was accomplished either during this dream or afterwards by following the instructions of the god. The pilgrim then made a thank offering and departed from the Asklepieion. Aristides' pilgrimage radically diverged from this pattern: the god kept him at the sanctuary in Pergamon for two years, occasionally sending him out on 'mini-pilgrimages' to a variety of locations. The accounts of these journeys in Books Two and Three emphasise (and self-dramatise) Aristides' extraordinary suffering and the miraculous nature of the god's cures. Through sacred travel, and already through literary composition ordered by the god, Aristides' series of illnesses are cured. The text describes a series of gruelling treatments which literally leave the marks of this divine favour on Aristides' body. For example, Asklepios disfigures Aristides' body with a large tumour in his groin by forbidding him to remove it by surgery or drugs (XLVII.63); he makes Aristides' body extremely thin by prescribing fasting and vomiting (XLVII.59); he makes Aristides' body change colour by ordering him to bathe in the freezing streams in the winter (XLVIII.53); he alters the appearance of his body by ordering him to smear it with mud and display himself in the sanctuary (XLIX.24), by ordering him to wear only a light shirt in winter and walk barefoot in the snow (XLVIII.78–80), and by ordering him not to bathe for five years (XLVII.59); he pierces his body to let the blood flow by ordering phlebotomies (XLVIII.47–48, XLIX.34); and he penetrates it by prescribing enemas (XLIX.34).

The narrative pattern of illness and miraculous recovery enacts the long-term nature of Aristides' pilgrimage to Asklepios. Although the theme of oratory is present in the first three books, eventually in Books Four and Five it takes centre stage. The god orders Aristides to begin to practise oratory again; although he thinks he is unable to declaim, he makes the attempt and he receives divine strength. Aristides then writes:

> But the god also ordered me to compose speeches, not only to contend extemporaneously, and besides sometimes to learn them word for word. And the matter afforded me much difficulty, for neither was I at

all able to conceive of any of the things which were to follow, nor could I trust his purpose – how could I have so much ease? – first I had to be saved. Yet, as it seems these were contrivances of his for the present moment, but at the same time he had better plans than salvation alone. Therefore he saved me by means worth more than the act of being saved. (L.29)

This passage presents the character of Aristides' developing understanding of the meaning of his illness. The illness, which had initially impeded his oratorical career, now appears to be a means of improving that oratorical skill. The narrative includes a statement to this effect made by Pardalas, a character described as 'the greatest expert of the Greeks of our time in the science of oratory', and thus ideally positioned to make such a judgement (L.27): 'He believed that I had become ill through some divine good fortune, so that by my association with the god, I might make this improvement.'

Throughout *The Sacred Tales*, Aristides presents himself as being in intimate and constant contact with Asklepios. But whereas in the first three books the locus for divine contact is Aristides' body, increasingly in Books Four and Five it is Aristides' oratory (his speeches and his writings). The text shifts from presenting Aristides' body and symptoms to presenting him engaged in literary composition. His visions continue to be of the god, but they are also of the greatest literary figures of Classical Antiquity, such as Demosthenes, Sophokles and Plato (L.57, 59–60). The text presents the god moving from Aristides' body to Aristides' words. *The Sacred Tales* itself as a literary composition demonstrated Aristides' talent, which was explicitly linked to the favour of the god.

The presentation of the god of healing as an oratorical mentor was unprecedented. Aristides apologises for this:

But it is necessary to try to make clear all of my oratorical career that pertains to the god and, as far as I can, to omit nothing of it. For it would be strange if both I and others would recount whatever cure he gave to my body even at home, but would pass by in silence those things which at the same time raised up my body, strengthened my soul, and increased the glory of my oratory. (LI.36)

The involvement of the body in the act of declamation and in the ability to travel to different cities did to some extent justify Aristides' linking of the themes of oratory and the body. However, in Book Four the narrative even presents the god of healing intervening to ensure that Aristides evaded civic duty: Asklepios directs Aristides' defence in court (L.63–104). Again, the unusual nature of this 'achievement' of the god is signalled apologetically in the text (L.63).

The author/pilgrim's understanding of his pilgrimage to Asklepios purports to develop and change in *The Sacred Tales* from a simple desire for bodily healing with a view to returning to the practice of oratory to long-term revelatory contact with the god designed to improve his oratorical skill, where the concepts of 'healing', 'sickness' and 'wellness' have been radically redefined. Repeated references to the intervention of Asklepios in directing the writing of *The Sacred Tales* suggests divine involvement in this narrative of revelation (XLVIII.4, L.68–69). The experience of a changing understanding of pilgrimage is evoked in the reader by the text's movement from descriptions of the minutiae of Aristides' stomach symptoms in Book One to accounts of dreams in Books Four and Five in which Plato and Sophokles come to visit and converse with him. The reader's expectations of pilgrimage to Asklepios are in effect challenged by this pattern and a new paradigm of pilgrimage is created for the uniquely favoured orator. Aristides' responsive reading of the landscape of his body leads him through a circuitous route of a series of illnesses and cures to his original goal: the resumption of his oratorical career. As the narrative shifts its focus from the body to oratory Aristides' image of a sick and suffering orator is transformed into that of a divinely favoured pilgrim orator. This transformation of identity is even reflected in a change of name: Asklepios bestows on Aristides the name Theodoros, which affirmed that his very existence was a 'gift of god' (L.53–54, 70).

Friar Felix Fabri, *Evagatorium in Terrae Sanctae*[9]

The *Evagatorium* describes Fabri's two pilgrimages to the Holy Land undertaken in 1480 and 1483–4. Although his dissatisfaction with the first pilgrimage was so great that it prompted him to make the second, on one level this first journey is presented as successful. Amidst great dangers, including illness, storms and lack of provisions during the journey, and the constant threat of capture by Turkish battleships, Fabri manages to get to Jerusalem, see the major sites of pilgrimage and return to Ulm. His fellow pilgrim Georg von Stein, son of the prefect of Upper Bavaria, accomplishes his goal of receiving a knighthood at the Church of the Holy Sepulchre. The text repeatedly emphasises that Fabri's safety was granted by God and that the accomplishment of the pilgrimage was in part due to divine intervention (e.g. 10A, 20B, 21B, 22A–B). At the end of the episode Fabri writes that this pilgrimage was more dangerous and difficult than the second and that it was a gift of God to return unscathed (22B).

Fabri's presentation of this pilgrimage as a failure involves the issue of his goal in undertaking it, his original model of pilgrimage. At the opening of the *Evagatorium*, Fabri discusses the merits of pilgrimage to the Holy Land and states that the aim of his pilgrimage was better to understand the Bible through viewing the sites of the Holy Land (9B). The failure of the pilgrimage is cast as a failure properly to view the sights and consequently a failure to develop a more profound understanding of the Bible.[10] He writes that the sightseeing was wholly unsatisfactory: he and his fellow pilgrims were not allowed to see certain sights, they saw others only once or in the failing light, and they were rushed from one sight to the other by guides and did not have enough time in Jerusalem (only nine days) (15B). The text dramatises this perfunctory sightseeing by describing not a single monument or aspect of the Holy Land (the description of the first pilgrimage is exclusively of the *journey*). Fabri writes that they ran around the holy places 'without understanding or feeling what they were' (23A). Although Fabri makes it clear that he wished to stay longer and that it was time pressure that prevented him from viewing the sights more carefully, he also portrays this failure in viewing as a failure of his response (both intellectual and emotional) to the landscape. He suggests that he was not able to relate it to the Bible and thus that his understanding of the Bible (the goal of the pilgrimage) failed.

The failure in viewing and understanding in Jerusalem is extended beyond the pilgrimage to the period after Fabri's return to Ulm:

So after I had returned to Ulm and began to think about the most holy sepulchre of our Lord and the manger wherein He lay, and the holy city of Jerusalem and the mountains which are round about it, the appearance, shape, and arrangements of these and of other holy places escaped from my mind, and the Holy Land and Jerusalem with its holy places appeared to me shrouded in a dark mist, as though I had beheld them in a dream; and I seemed to myself to know less about all the holy places than I did before I visited them, whence it happened that when I was questioned about the holy places I could give no distinct answers, nor could I write a clear description of my journey. (23A)

Fabri's inability to recall images of the sights, to feel an increased understanding of them, and to express this through the spoken and written word, confirms that he had made great efforts 'without receiving any fruit, consolation, or knowledge' (23B). Unlike Aristides (who, although he did not receive the health that he sought, nonetheless received oratorical instruction from the god), Fabri neither received the sights and knowledge he desired, nor was he given an alternative gift. The experience is presented as being so fruitless and negative that Fabri expresses doubts, both to himself and to others, about whether he had actually been to the Holy Land at all (23B).

Although the literary character of Fabri tries to excise the first pilgrimage from his history, Fabri the author does not excise it from the pilgrimage *narrative*. The description of the first pilgrimage in fact plays an important role in the *Evagatorium* because it is the background against which the second, successful, pilgrimage is set. But the first pilgrimage also provides the framework in which the character Fabri is seen to develop as he actively works through his disappointing experience and gives it new meaning. On his departure from Jerusalem he redefines the (failed) pilgrimage as a (successful) preamble to a second pilgrimage (16B). On his return to Ulm he makes an imaginative 'literary' pilgrimage to the Holy Land by collecting and reading all pilgrimage accounts he has access to:[11]

So I read everything on this subject which came into my hands; moreover I collected all the stories of the pilgrimages of the crusades, the tracts written by pilgrims, and the descriptions of the Holy Land, and read them with care; and the more I read the more my trouble increased, because by reading the accounts of others I learned how imperfect, superficial, irregular and confused my own pilgrimage had been. (1B; 23B)

In this process he constructs an ideal pilgrimage to the Holy Land, by means of the accounts of other pilgrims; in the light of this model the failure of his own pilgrimage is confirmed.

This 'literary' pilgrimage, which enables Fabri to construct a more specific sense of what his pilgrimage should be like, is then followed by a real one to the Holy Land in order to *see* what he had only read about (1B). The success of this pilgrimage is dramatised in the narrative: Fabri's viewing on this occasion is shown to be successful not only by means of detailed descriptions of the monuments and landscape, but also by means of relating those sights to the stories of the Bible. An important aspect of this process is a notional comparison of the appearance of the sight with its appearance in Biblical times (e.g. 124b–129b on the Holy Sepulchre then and at the time of the passion of Christ). Viewing and interpreting thus act as a bridge between the physical landscape and the imaginative landscape, constructed both by the Bible and by the pilgrimage narratives which Fabri had read. The success of this pilgrimage is confirmed by a careful recording of the indulgences received by visiting the sights: although Fabri would also have received indulgences on the first pilgrimage, the text chooses to deploy this symbol of spiritual achievement for the second pilgrimage, not the first.

Fabri's second pilgrimage is characterised by new visions and perspectives. These occur most obviously in relation to the biblical landscape and text but also in relation to the city of Ulm and to the character of Fabri as constructed by his text. On his return, Fabri hardly recognises his home city, the appearance of which has been drastically altered by new buildings. He himself is recognised at his monastery by a dog (a story surely meant to recall the dog Argos' recognition of the returning hero in Homer's *Odyssey* XVII 1.290–327) (230B). His appearance, however, is greatly altered both by his beard and his pilgrim's clothes. Although, as a Dominican friar, he is obliged to shave off the beard, which he feels conveys a sense of his pilgrim's courage and experience, he does manage to retain his pilgrim's clothes under his habit (231A). His transformation into a new person is neatly reflected by his description of his reception at the monastery: to his fellow monks, who had received false reports of his death, he appeared to live again (231A). These hints of a changed Fabri at the end of the narrative should be seen in the context of a statement at the beginning of the narrative that gaining a deeper understanding of the Bible would help Fabri to become a better preacher. In other words, the goal of the pilgrimage is explicitly presented in the context of the person and vocation of Fabri. It should also be seen in the wider context of the prominence of the author/pilgrim throughout the *Evagatorium* and in particular of the self-conscious fashioning of his person as 'Frater Felix Fabri' and 'FFF'.[12] There were alternatives: Fabri also wrote a narrative of the pilgrimage in German, in which he called himself Felix Schmidt.[13] Fabri's location of identity in his name is specifically related to his interaction with the landscape in a passage from the second pilgrimage. Prompted by the location of St Felix's birthplace in Egyptian Thebes, Fabri writes that he himself is linked to the saint because he was born in Zurich where the saint was martyred and 'reborn' in the baptismal waters over the tomb of the saint, and because he was given the saint's name (140A). There is a similarity in the way that Fabri and Aristides discuss their religious names in these texts and link their pilgrimages to their vocations, in effect fashioning themselves as pilgrim-preacher and pilgrim-orator respectively.

The prologue of the *Evagatorium* discusses the nature of the virtuous pilgrim and justifies the practice of pilgrimage to the Holy Land, largely drawing on scriptural sources (3B–9A). Fabri writes that the pilgrim who follows in the footsteps of Jesus and of the original pilgrims (the Apostles) will not be able to accomplish all that he wishes (5A–B). In other words, a degree of failure is anticipated. The process of responding to this experience and reinterpreting it is encapsulated in the narrative of Fabri's first pilgrimage. The truly 'virtuous pilgrim', whose definition is fleshed out in the course of the narrative, is revealed to be the one who manages not only to see the sights (itself an achievement) but also to respond to them – to understand them and to remember them. The landscape (of the Holy Land and of Ulm), the sacred text and the person of Fabri are all transformed in this process. The presentation of pilgrimage as a process of response in the *Evagatorium* is reflected in the life of Fabri who, before he died, had managed to get permission for a third pilgrimage to the Holy Land.[14]

Pierre Loti, *Un pèlerin d'Angkor*[15]

While his ship was docked in Saigon in late November 1901, the French naval officer/writer Pierre Loti made a journey up the Mekong river to visit the ancient temples of Angkor. Although his journey only lasted a few days, the narrative *Un pèlerin d'Angkor* spans Loti's whole life, beginning with a chapter relating events of his childhood, then a series of chapters on the journey, situated in a relative chronology 'approximately thirty-five years later', and finally a chapter dated October 1910, in which Loti explicitly looks back and contemplates his life, which is said to be ending (though in fact he died thirteen years later). In addition to this feature of retrospective autobiographical interpretation, the first chapter opens with a statement of Loti's foreknowledge of his life, including his pilgrimage to Angkor (1991: 1181), and the narrative frequently looks forward and back in time. Despite these programmatic features, the narrative depicts an unfolding experience of pilgrimage, and only in the last chapter does Loti express his final verdict on the value and meaning of the pilgrimage, and indeed of his other travels.

The narrative opens and closes at Loti's family home in Rochefort. Loti describes himself as a child and then finally as an old man in the same room, his 'museum', 'where I had gathered a collection of shells, rare-plumaged birds, Oceanic arms and ornaments, everything that conjured up distant countries for me' (Loti (1991): 1181–82). This physical attempt to construct a picture of the world is the backdrop for Loti's 'real' experience of it. The close connection of the landscape of this exotic world and Loti's autobiographical sense is reflected in the description of this museum in another narrative: in *Prime Jeunesse*, an autobiographical narrative first published in 1919, the objects are distinguished by their connection to Loti's relatives, for example, 'little antiquated Chinese ornaments from great uncles who were navigators' (Loti (1999): 353–54). The life of adventures and travels which the museum foretells the child

Loti is again envisaged in explicitly personal terms: it is not the exotic world that he imagines, but his transformation into a hero or pirate (1991: 1182). Although Loti predicts change to his person, in the imaginary scene of his return his family home remains basically unchanged, with the exception of the loot he will have brought back with him (imagined as 'precious stones from Golconda' and 'fantastic loot', 1991: 1182). The description of Loti's real return in the final chapter picks up the theme of change (or the lack of it) to his person and to his home, and describes the very different 'loot' that he comes back with.

In contrast to Aristides' and Fabri's religious pilgrimages, Loti's pilgrimage to Angkor is initially envisaged as part of an open-ended series of 'secular' travels of discovery of the world and the self. The first chapter also connects the inception of the journey to another personal and nonreligious feature, the death of Loti's older brother in Indo-China: while leafing through the latter's papers, the young Loti is said to have seen the engraving of Angkor in a copy of the *Revue Coloniale*, which inspired his desire to see the temples. Loti's orientalising discourse constructs a journey of cultural exploration to 'the ruins of Angkor' and insists on the extinction of the Khmer culture which created Angkor (1991: 1218).[16] In contemporary Indo-China he sees only traces of the culture which 'really' interests him:

> The little Cambodia of today, the repository and preserver of complicated rites the significance of which is no longer known is a last remnant of that vast empire of the Khmers, which for more than five hundred years now has been extinguished under the silence of trees and mosses. (1991: 1198)

All this is asserted in the face of numerous references to contemporary Buddhist religious activity, including pilgrimage to Angkor (1991: 1205, 1209, 1211, 1213). Although Loti implicitly contrasts this to his own kind of journey, he nevertheless styles himself a 'pilgrim' in the title and makes several references to the fact that he stayed in pilgrims' huts both on his journey and at Angkor (1991: 1195, 1203, 1220). The distinction between secular journey and religious pilgrimage is challenged in the last chapter, where Loti writes that what he has gained from his personal pilgrimage to

Angkor and from his travels to other places in his capacity as naval officer is a deeper religious understanding of God (1991: 1233–4).[17] The emerging secular/religious tension is one aspect of Loti's presentation of a developing understanding of the nature of his pilgrimage.

The disjunction between the pilgrimage Loti had imagined and the one that he actually experienced is repeatedly expressed in the narrative. This disjunction is expressed in relation to the image of the temple of Angkor Wat that inspired the pilgrimage and to his general expectations of what he would see and feel as a pilgrim (1991: 1208, 1213). These are the descriptions of Loti's first and last views of Angkor:

> Yes! I recognise them at once. They are indeed the towers in the old picture which had so troubled me once upon a time, on an April evening, in my childhood museum. I am in the presence of mysterious Angkor! Yet somehow I do not feel the emotion that I should have expected. It is probably too late in life, and I have seen too many of these remains of the great past, too many temples, too many palaces, too many ruins. Besides it is all so blurred, as it were, under the glare of the daylight; it is difficult to see it because it is too bright. And, above all, midday is drawing near with its lassitude, its invincible somnolence ... (1991: 1194)
>
> I turn therefore to take a last look at Angkor. This pilgrimage, which since my childhood I had hoped to make, is now a thing accomplished, and has fallen into the past, as one day will fall my own brief human existence, and I shall never see again, rising into the sky, those great strange towers. I cannot even, this last time, follow them for long with my eyes, for immediately the forest closed round us, suddenly ushering in the twilight. (1991: 1220)

The failure of the real pilgrimage to Angkor to match the imaginary one is expressed, as it is in Fabri's *Evagatorium*, as a literal failure of viewing related to the light. The first passage also identifies Loti's failure to respond to the sight of the temple, which does fit the image of the engraving seen in childhood. The disjunction between the imaginary and the real pilgrimage is also expressed by constant evocations of what Angkor would have looked like during the height of the Khmer civilisation and the reality of the 'ruins' (1991: 1197, 1205, 1212–14). Whereas in the *Evagatorium* the evocation of the appearance of sights in biblical times confirms their authenticity and their relationship to the biblical text, in Loti's text the evocation of the appearance of 'Khmer Angkor' seems to highlight the distance between the pilgrim's experience and 'the real thing'. Loti even makes an imaginary 'archaeological' reconstruction of the temple of the Bayon (1991: 1217). The narrative of these disappointed expectations in effect constructs images of Loti's imaginary Angkor and at the same time describes the pilgrim's process of responding to the reality of the landscape.

Following the arrival at Angkor, the narrative describes Loti's 'mini-pilgrimages' to the temples of Angkor Wat and the Bayon. During the course of four viewings under different weather and light conditions, Loti's impression of Angkor develops. For example, on his first visit to the Bayon at dusk the smiling faces of the *bodhisattva* of compassion on the towers (mistakenly identified by Loti as 'Brahma') are described as threatening, whereas on his second morning visit they appear heavily ironic (1991: 1200, 1216). And in the course of one visit to Angkor Wat, Loti's understanding of the layout and meaning of the temple is shown to develop: as he climbs up to the top of the temple his initial impression of architectural disorder is replaced by an appreciation of architectural regularity and proportion, seen as symbolic of a religious harmony (1991: 1206, 1212). Two features are constantly reiterated: the strangeness of this culture and its extinction (1991: 1202–3, 1218–9, 1198). Only on Loti's fourth and final viewing of Angkor Wat does he express a sense of increasing familiarity and intimacy with the sculptural figures (1991: 1219). These episodes construct a pattern of development of the author/pilgrim's relationship to the landscape through a process of engagement and response.

But Loti's desire to find Khmer culture is fundamentally frustrated at the ruins of Angkor: he sees only stone Apsaras, and wonders about the real models who died many hundred years ago (1991: 1201). The tantalising image of the beautiful stone breasts of the Apsaras recurs in descriptions of the temples. On his departure from Angkor, Loti predicts that at the royal palace at Phnom Penh he would see Apsaras 'no longer dead, with these fixed smiles of stone, but in the fullness of life and youth, no longer with these breasts of rigid sandstone, but with palpitating breasts of flesh, and wearing veritable tiaras of gold, and sparkling with veritable jewels' (1991: 1220). At the unexpected 'apotheosis' of his pilgrimage (1991: 1232) the stone breasts which are caressed by pilgrims at Angkor (1991: 1211) are transformed into the dancers' real breasts which are lingered over by the eyes of another 'Angkor pilgrim' (1991: 1227–8, 1229). The frieze from Angkor Wat depicting scenes of Buddhist mythology comes alive in Phnom Penh at the real culmination of pilgrimage in search of a colonial vision of ancient Khmer culture:

> We are in the midst of the Ramayana, and the same performances were once enacted, no doubt, at Angkor Thom, the same costumes worn there. This evening we are able to imagine, better than ever before, what were the splendours of the legendary town. Epochs we thought were gone forever come to life again before our eyes. ... In spite of its diminished outward appearances, this fallen Cambodian race has remained the Khmer people, the people which astonished Asia of olden times by its pomp and mysticism. (1991: 1229)

The accomplishment of the ostensible goal of Loti's pilgrimage to see 'the evening star rise over the great ruins of Angkor' (1991: 1200) has now, at the end of the journey narrative, been superseded by a new realisation of the goal of pilgrimage – the evocation of genuine living Khmer culture. The pilgrimage narrative constructs this story of Loti's developing understanding of his pilgrimage through his response to the landscape and sculpture of Angkor and to the female body.

The pilgrimage to see the ruins of Angkor and Khmer civilisation is thus successfully accomplished. The final chapter, however, depicts a dejected Loti back in Rochefort in his unchanged childhood 'museum'. The narrative constructs a homecoming and final assessment of the pilgrimage ten years after the journey to Angkor. The narrative asserts the importance of working out the final outcome of the pilgrimage, of identifying 'the fantastic loot'. The retrospective meditation on the pilgrimage is used autobiographically to explore the course of Loti's life, which is said to be coming to an end. It is precisely the lack of change in Loti as a person – his failure to become a 'hero' or a 'pirate' – that are presented as infinitely disappointing in this final autobiographical assessment. The first chapter presented the child Loti's desire to transform himself into a hero through exploration of the world and in particular of the exotic 'colonies'. In the final chapter his travels are said to have failed to transform Loti, who is different to the child only in his limited life expectancy (1991: 1233). Whereas in the fifteenth-century *Evagatorium* the failed pilgrimage has to be superseded by a second successful one, the modern narrative of personal pilgrimage can accommodate failure at the end.[18] It is only in the very last section of the narrative that Loti is presented working out what he has extracted from his travels over the world: he tentatively identifies 'a kind of education which does not yet suffice, but has brought already an outline of serenity' (1991: 1233). The text dramatises the process of gaining a deeper religious understanding, of recognising a compassionate God in the many guises in which He is worshipped around the world. Although this passage refers to all Loti's travels, the smiles of pardon of the Buddhist statues at Angkor are specifically mentioned (1991: 1233). The exploration of another belief system and the achievement of some kind of affinity with it is a distinctively modern feature, which contrasts with the pilgrimages of Aristides and Fabri to the 'centres' of their religions.

Although on one level Loti fails to transform himself into the hero/pirate through world travel, on another level his identity as traveller and pilgrim is affirmed in the course of the pilgrimage narrative. The exploration of the self and the landscape are intimately connected in Loti's writings. This feature is also reflected in Loti's self-fashioning in his life: his *nom de plume* is derived from the landscape of his homeland (his family came from the island of Saint *Pierre* d'Oleron) and was ceremoniously adopted in Tahiti. His identity was collapsed into the identity of foreign countries in the photographs of him dressed up in exotic costumes (Figure 1). Another aspect of Loti's use of his journeys into foreign lands for self-fashioning and self-definition was his use of an increased sexual freedom, in particular for homosexual affairs. Some of these journeys of sexual exploration are described in Loti's writings, such as 'Aziyadé', a thinly disguised autobiographical novel (published in 1879) relating a young Frenchman's love affairs in Constantinople. A portrait of Loti by Félix Vallotton succinctly combines these twin ideas of sexual exploration and the exploration of the landscape of the world (Figure 2):

Figure 1

Figure 2

the toy boat, military sword and miniature colonial subjects he clutches point to Loti's naval career and travels, while the dress he wears hints at his sexual explorations in the direction of bisexuality and transvestism.

Conclusion

The narrative pattern of a developing understanding of pilgrimage suggests that retrospectively the authors/pilgrims understood the active process of response to be an important feature of their different pilgrimages.[19] In the texts I have explored, this involves a renegotiation of what the pilgrims/authors originally desired to attain on their pilgrimage and what they actually felt that they did attain in the event. Aristides desired his illness to be cured in order that he could resume his oratorical career; in the event his series of illnesses continued to bring him into contact with the healing deity who gave him only temporary cures, but through this ongoing contact fashioned him as a divinely favoured pilgrim orator. Loti desired to fulfil his childhood wish to see the ruins of the temples of Angkor, which he had seen depicted in an engraving in a copy of the *Revue Coloniale*; in the event he is disappointed when he sees them because they do not bring to life a sense of the ancient Khmer civilisation, but instead the culmination of the pilgrimage turns out to be the spectacle of live dancers at the royal palace at Phnom Penh performing traditional ancient Khmer dances. In both these cases the deep desire of the author/pilgrim which prompted the pilgrimage is fulfilled in very different ways to what was expected, and the texts describe the process of bridging the gap between expectation and actual experience. In the case of Fabri's first pilgrimage to the Holy Land, his desire to see the sights, to gain a deepened knowledge of the Bible and become a better preacher is disappointed, and the narrative presents no alternative achievement. The narrative depicts Fabri redefining this pilgrimage as a preamble to a second pilgrimage in which the desire to view the biblical sights, to enrich his understanding of the Bible and then to communicate this understanding as a pilgrim writer and a preacher, is eventually fulfilled.

The theme that I have traced in the three texts is, of course, operating in very different cultural contexts and traditions of pilgrimage. It also taps into very different notions of self and personhood. Whereas the prominence of the authorial persona and his or her emotions was not an unusual feature in early twentieth-century literature, such as Loti's *Un pèlerin d'Angkor*, it was unusual in literature of the second century AD. It is perhaps not a coincidence that many Classical scholars intensely dislike Aristides and judge him to be self-obsessed. Certainly his character in *The Sacred Tales* is far more prominent than that of the periegete/pilgrim Pausanias in the *Description of Greece*. Perhaps *The Sacred Tales* can be located not only at the end of a Classical tradition of religious and travel literature, but also at the beginning of a tradition which would eventually be identified as Christian, and which increasingly focused on the interiority of the person. One way in which this operated in the context of pilgrimage writing was the intimate linking – even subordination – of the exterior landscape to the interior self. The description of the person's journey through the real landscape provided the means to effect this transition. In *The Sacred Tales*, the journey and its effect on the body and spirit of Aristides is an innovative and remarkable feature; in the *Evagatorium* it is an accepted topos of the genre. Although during the course of his travels around Greece Pausanias also famously arrives at a new understanding of the significance of the traditional religious myths which he once treated with scepticism (8.8.3), this process is not presented in the light of Pausanias' personal development. With *The Sacred Tales*, however, we can perhaps identify hints of a travel discourse which eventually came to be closely associated with a Protestant Christian tradition of pilgrimage writing that entirely collapsed the outer landscape into the internal landscape of the soul (for example, John Bunyan's *The Pilgrim's Progress*).

In the three texts I have examined, the meaning of the pilgrimage is explored by means of putting the character of the author/pilgrim within the framework of the pilgrimage narrative. We can see an aesthetic parallel in the 'real' pilgrimage process as the pilgrim places himself or herself in the physical framework of the pilgrimage shrine. Although there is no absolute line of demarcation, one feature which distinguishes pilgrimage cross-culturally from more open-ended travel is the operation of (different) *specific* models of the practice and meaning of pilgrimage. These models operate on a conceptual level and set out what a pilgrimage should achieve and what it should feel like. They are often mediated through texts and images generated by past pilgrims or, in the case of Christianity, by its canonical text, the Bible. The discrepancy between the pilgrimage ideal and the reality gives rise to the process of renegotiating the meaning and value of the pilgrimage for each pilgrim personally, within the pilgrimage tradition in which he or she is operating. It is an active process, which constantly challenges and recasts the pilgrimage tradition itself. It is an aspect of this process that we can identify in the act of writing about pilgrimage in general, and in particular in the elaboration of the theme of the pilgrim/author's changing understanding of pilgrimage. So in the *Evagatorium* and *Un pèlerin d'Angkor*, both Fabri and Loti try to relate what they see to the descriptions which had inspired their pilgrimages in the first place: in the case of Fabri the description was textual (the Bible and past pilgrimage narratives) and in the case of Loti it was visual (the engraving of the temple of Angkor Wat in the *Revue Coloniale*). The pilgrimage narratives describe a process of reading the physical landscape in the light of these 'texts' and in turn of rereading these 'texts' in the light of the landscape. At the end of the second, successful, pilgrimage Fabri returns to the Bible and is able to correlate the sights of the Holy Land to the stories of the Bible (1B); and at the end of his pilgrimage Loti returns to his family home and looks at and reinterprets the engraving of Angkor (1991: 1231–33). These descriptions of mutual transformation of landscape and 'text' are in turn connected to the personal transformation of the author/pilgrim: Fabri's enriched knowledge of the Bible makes him a better preacher and Loti's new understanding of the universal nature of God and the human predicament enhances his image as an intellectual twentieth-century traveller. Ultimately, through the medium of the pilgrimage narrative, all three pilgrims renegotiate the question of what it means to be a pilgrim in the light of the initial disappointment of their pilgrimage ideal. Within these narratives the authorial self emerges as the locus for this process.

Notes

1 Morinis (1992: 1–28).
2 On *curiositas* and pilgrimage see Zacher (1976).
3 On pilgrimage and tourism see Cohen (1992).

4 See Elsner and Rubiés (1999: 1–56).

5 *The Sacred Tales* contain a number of references to events which occurred many years after the pilgrimage to Asklepios (AD 145–47); on the basis of these it is thought that Aelius Aristides wrote *The Sacred Tales* AD c.170. In the *Evagatorium*, Fabri writes that he was unable to write about his pilgrimage after the first journey to the Holy Land, which took place from 14 April to 16 November 1480. After his second pilgrimage to the Holy Land and to St. Catherine's monastery at Sinai (13 April 1483 to 30 January 1484) he wrote the narrative of both journeys. Masson has argued that, on the basis of certain references to political events in the text, it is possible to give a *terminus post quem* of 1494 for the composition of the *Evagatorium* (Fabri 1975: vii–viii); more recently Meyers and Chareyron have suggested on the basis of the same references a date between 1484 and 1488 (Fabri 2000: xvii–xviii). Loti's voyage to Angkor occurred in 1901 and *Un pèlerin d'Angkor* was written in 1911 and published in 1912 (Loti 1991: 1179).

6 Pearcy (1988).

7 Loti (1989).

8 For interpretation of *The Sacred Tales* as autobiographical narrative see Bompaire (1993) and Quet (1993); on the sick and suffering body King (1999) and Perkins (1995: 173–90); on dreaming see Cox Miller (1994: 184–204); on pilgrimage see Rutherford (1999) and Petsalis-Diomidis (2001: 70–163); on the theme of documentation see Pearcy (1988); on literary style see Weiss (1998: 47–73); on the Roman/Greek cultural interface see Swain (1998: 260–74). See also Festugière (1954: 85–104), Dodds (1965: 41–45), Brown (1978: 27–53), Behr (1968), Cortés-Copete (1995: 55–86), Jones (1998). Translations of *The Sacred Tales* are from Aristides (1981); all references are to the original text, Aristides (1958).

9 On the *Evagatorium in Terrae Sanctae* see Prescott (1954), Tinguely (1997) and Williams (1998: 37–42). Translations of the *Evagatorium in Terrae Sanctae* are from Fabri (1896–7); all references are to the original text, Fabri (1843–9).

10 On the importance of visuality, interactive viewing and the 'eye of faith' in Late Antique narratives of pilgrimage to the Holy Land, see Frank (2000: 102–33).

11 Coleman and Elsner (1995: 92, 210).

12 Fabri (2000: xix, xxix–xxx).

13 Fabri (1999: 59–61); Fabri (1975: v–x); Fabri (2000: xviii–xix).

14 Fabri (2000: xviii).

15 All translations of *Un pèlerin d'Angkor* are from Loti (1996); references are to the original text, Loti (1991).

16 Said (1978); Hargreaves (1981: 21–85).

17 Cohen (1992); Coleman and Elsner (1995: 213).

18 On the failure of the pilgrimage ideal after the Renaissance see Elsner and Rubiés (1999: 29–56).

19 Coleman and Elsner (1995: 206).

References

Aristides, A. (1958) *Aelii Aristidis Smyrnaei quae supersunt omnia* Volumen II

Orationes XVII-LIII Continens, ed.B. Keil. Berlin: Weidmannos.

—— (1981) *The Complete Works of P. Aelius Aristides,* trans. C.A. Behr, Volume II Orations XVII–LIII. Leiden: Brill.

Behr, C.A. (1968) *Aelius Aristides and The Sacred Tales.* Amsterdam: A.M. Hakkert.

Blanch, L. (1983) *Pierre Loti: Portrait of an Escapist.* London: Collins.

Bompaire J. (1993) 'Quatre styles d'autobiographie au IIe siècle après J.-C: Aelius Aristide, Lucien, Marc-Aurèle, Galien', in M.-F. Baslez, P. Hoffmann and L. Pernot (eds) *L'invention de l'autobiographie d'Hésiode à saint Augustin.* Paris: Presses de l'école Normale Supérieure, pp. 199–209.

Brown, P. (1978) *The Making of Late Antiquity.* Cambridge, M.A.: Harvard University Press.

Cohen, E. (1992) 'Pilgrimage and Tourism: Convergence and Divergence' in E. Morinis (ed.) *Sacred Journeys: The Anthropology of Pilgrimage.* Westport, C.T.: Greenwood Publishing Group, pp. 47–61.

Coleman, S. and Elsner, J. (1995) *Pilgrimage: Past and Present in the World Religions.* Cambridge, M.A.: Harvard University Press.

Cortés-Copete, J. (1995) *Elio Aristides: un sofista griego en el Imperio Romano.* Madrid: Clasicas.

Cox Miller, P. (1994) *Dreams in Late Antiquity: Studies in the Imagination of a Culture.* Princeton: Princeton University Press.

Dodds, E.R. (1965) *Pagan and Christian in an Age of Anxiety.* Cambridge: Cambridge University Press.

Elsner, J.and Rubiés, J.-P. (1999) (eds) *Voyages & Visions: Towards a Cultural History of Travel.* London: Reaktion Books.

Fabri, F. (1843–9) *Evagatorium in Terrae Sanctae, Arabiae et Egypti Peregrinationem,* Vols I–III, ed. C.D. Hassler. Stuttgart: Sumtibus Societatis Literariae Stuttgardiensis.

—— (1896–7) *The Wanderings of Friar Felix Fabri,* trans. A. Stewart. London: Palestine Pilgrim's Society, t.VII-X.

—— (1975) *Voyage en Egypte de Felix Fabri, 1483,* trans. Jacques Masson. Paris-Le Caire: Institut Français d'Archéologie Orientale du Caire.

—— (1999) *Felix Fabri, Die Sionpilger (1492),* ed. C. Wieland. Berlin: Erich Schmidt Verlag.

—— (2000) *Les errances de Frère Félix, pèlerin en Terre sainte, en Arabie et en Egypte (1480–1483)* trans. Jean Meyers and Nicole Chareyon. Montpelier: Université Paul-Valéry.

Festugière, A.-J. (1954) *Personal Religion among the Greeks.* Berkeley, C.A.: University of California Press.

Frank, G. (2000) *The Memory of the Eyes: Pilgrims to Living Saints in Christian Late Antiquity.* Berkeley, C.A.: University of California Press.

Hargreaves, A. (1981) *The Colonial Experience in French Fiction: A Study of Pierre Loti, Ernest Psichari and Pierre Mille.* London: The Macmillan Press.

Jones, C. (1998) 'Aelius Aristides and the Asklepieion', in H. Koester (ed.) *Pergamon, Citadel of the Gods.* Harvard Theological Studies 46 (Pennsylvania), pp.63–76.

King, H. (1999) 'Chronic Pain and the Creation of Narrative', in J. Porter (ed.) *Constructions of the Classical Body.* Ann Arbor: University of Michigan Press, pp. 269–86.

Loti, P. (1989) *Un pèlerin d'Angkor,* ed. Yves La Prairie. Paris: La Nompareille.

—— (1991) *Voyages (1972–1913),* ed. C. Martin. Paris: Robert Laffont.

———— (1996) *A Pilgrimage to Angkor*, trans. W.P. Baines W.P. and M. Smithies. Bangkok: Silkworm Books.

———— (1999) *Le Roman d'un enfant* suivi de *Prime jeunesse*, ed. B. Vercier. Paris: Gallimard.

Morinis, E. (ed.) (1992) *Sacred Journeys: The Anthropology of Pilgrimage*. Westport, C.T.: Greenwood Publishing Group.

Pausanias (1988–1995) *Description of Greece* Vols V ed. W.H.S. Jones et al. Cambridge M.A.: Loeb Classical Library.

Pearcy, L. (1988) 'Theme, Dream and Narrative: Reading the *Sacred Tales* of Aelius Aristides', *Transactions of the American Philological Association* 118: 377–91.

Perkins, J. (1995) *The Suffering Self: Pain and Narrative Representation in the Early Christian Era*. London: Routledge.

Petsalis-Diomidis, A. (2001) 'Truly Beyond Miracles: The Body and Healing Pilgrimage in the Eastern Roman Empire in the Second Century AD', PhD thesis, The Courtauld Institute of Art, University of London.

Prescott, H. (1954) *Jerusalem Journey: Pilgrimage to the Holy Land in the Fifteenth Century*. London: Eyre and Spottiswoode.

Quet, M.-H. (1993) 'Parler de soi pour louer son dieu: le cas d'Aelius Aristide (du journal intime de ses nuits aux *Discours Sacrés* en l' honneur du dieu Asklépios)', in M.-F. Baslez, P. Hoffmann and L. Pernot (eds) *L'invention de l'autobiographie d'Hésiode à saint Augustin*. Paris: Presses de l'école Normale Supérieure, pp.211–51.

Rutherford, I. (1999) '*To the Land of Zeus …*: Patterns of Pilgrimage in Aelius Aristides', *Aevum Antiquum* 12: 133–48.

Said, E. (1978) *Orientalism*. London: Routledge and Kegan Paul.

Swain, S. (1998) *Hellenism and Empire*. Oxford: Oxford University Press.

Tinguely, Fr. (1997) 'Janus en terre sainte: la figure du pèlerin curieux à la Renaissance', in *Homo Viator Le Voyage de la vie (XVe–XXe siècles), Revue des Sciences Humaines no 245 Janvier-Mars 1997*: 51–65.

Weiss, C. (1998) 'Literary Turns: The Representation of Conversion in Aelius Aristides' *Hieroi Logoi* and in Apuleius' *Metamorphoses*' PhD thesis, Yale University.

Williams, W. (1998) *Pilgrimage and Narrative in the French Renaissance: 'The Undiscovered Country'*. Oxford: Clarendon Press.

Zacher, C. (1976) *Curiosity and Pilgrimage: The Literature of Discovery in Fourteenth-century England*. Baltimore, M.D.: The Johns Hopkins University Press.

Bowing Down to Wood and Stone: One Way to be a Pilgrim

Charles Lock
University of Copenhagen

The title of this essay alludes to the familiar Protestant hymn, whose imperial reach stretches from the Arctic to the Equator, from a Danish colony to a British one. Rhetorically, the hymn's 'inverted apostrophe' is extended by anaphora: these lands are not addressed by us, as 'O Greenland, O India'; rather, they and their barbaric people call us; they solicit our colonial attentions:

> From Greenland's icy mountains,
>   From India's coral strand,
> Where Afric's sunny fountains
>   Roll down their golden sand;
> From many an ancient river,
>   From many a palmy plain,
> They call us to deliver
>   Their land from error's chain.
>
> What though the spicy breezes
>   Blow soft o'er Ceylon's isle,
> Though every prospect pleases
>   And only man is vile:
> In vain with lavish kindness
>   The gifts of God are strown,
> The heathen in his blindness
>   Bows down to wood and stone!
>
> (*English Hymnal* 1933: 709 (no. 547))

Written in 1817 by Reginald Heber (1783–1826), a Shropshire vicar who would only later (in 1823) be consecrated Bishop of Calcutta, this hymn encapsulates certain Protestant prejudices, and sets up a number of significant oppositions. Before we attend to 'wood and stone' and the action of prostration, however, we should note the 'prospect' that pleases: the beauty of that exotic world where the gifts of God are so lavishly strewn, yet so erroneously received by the natives. Their 'blindness' is not only of a moral or spiritual order, but may stand also for the shortsightedness which prevents appreciation of God's gifts arranged in a pleasing prospect. The antithesis is implied: on the one hand, the prospect, on the other hand, idols of wood and stone. On the one hand, distance, on the other, proximity. (Hands are quite inadequate as figures for optical antitheses.) For a prospect, as we know from landscape art, or from the novels of Heber's contemporary, Jane Austen (1775–1817), is that which is arranged according to perspective: that which constitutes the precise position from which it can best, or properly, be seen. And that position is, of course, one of authority, mastery, possession: a prospect confers optical propriety. (The opening chapter of Christopher Hussey's *The Picturesque* from 1927, 'The Prospect,' is still to be recommended.) In the nineteenth century it is England, or the English eye, that affords the viewpoint by which the global prospect is constituted, and the missionary obligation laid down. By contrast, to prostrate is to be vulnerable; bowing down, one surrenders distance and optical mastery in order to attain proximity to the object. To be unsighted, to have no clear object of vision, forms no small part of abjection and subservience.

The relation between perspective and property is easily traced through the Quattrocento: the development of Renaissance perspective leads to the shift from fresco to panel-painting and thence to the portable canvas. It is on canvas that pictorial art is commodified and dispatched into the market-place. Such a portable painting carries with it, at a distance, the proper point-of-view: the space around the painting is coordinated in terms of the painting, and becomes part of what is owned. It is prestigious to own a landscape on the grand scale, because one must own a living-space in which it can be properly viewed: not only a wall of the right size, but a room of adequate dimensions. The more extensive the pictorial vista, the larger the implied space of viewing. This implied space of viewing has much to do with the nexus of capitalism and Protestantism, with the distance that keeps us from the object, and that keeps us pure, uncontaminated by contact; and with the property that is owned and controlled from a distance. And the value thus newly inscribed in distance goes some way to explain the aesthetic framing of England's far-flung colonies.

Heber's hymn is thus representative of its moment, in its opposition between the optic and the haptic, between the prospect to be viewed and the artefact to be idolized. We may also suppose that this moment is charged not only with imperial confidence, but also with anxieties, and one in particular. In the nineteenth century Protestants began to go on pilgrimages. It is often said that this occurred for reasons that had less to do with theology than with Thomas Cook. Yet Thomas Cook was responding to a demand clearly articulated in theological terms. Protestants wanted to go to the Holy Land, and from the early nineteenth century did so in increasing numbers. We think of their travels in terms of pilgrimage, yet it was a pilgrimage grounded in something other than the devotional mode that had inspired the cults which we associate with Canterbury or Rome, Santiago de Compostela or Walsingham.

Protestant pilgrimage in the nineteenth century is the expression of devotion modified by historicism. History and archaeology were the disciplines that could now confirm the actuality of the events and places of the Bible: 'Palestine, it may be said, was rediscovered by Edward Robinson in 1841.' (Elliott-Binns 1956: 102); 'Robinson had published his Biblical Researches in Palestine between 1838 and 1852' (Daniel 1950: 220) It is from the mid-nineteenth century that Protestants would undertake the pilgrimage, not to worship, but to test and confirm the topographical truths of scripture. Yet for all the curiosity about particular sites, the religious sentiment, of worship or devotion, tends to find expression not in precise local recognitions but in broad terms of landscape. This is evident as early as 1834 when Robert Curzon deployed the discourse of the sublime, to which the tourist as aesthete was accustomed, as the expression of pious yearning:

> As our train of horses surmounted each succeeding eminence, every one was eager to be the first who should catch a glimpse of the Holy City ... . With one accord our whole party drew their bridles, and stood still to gaze for the first time upon this renowned and sacred city.

It is not easy to describe the sensations which fill the breast of a Christian when, after a long and toilsome journey, he first beholds this, the most interesting and venerated spot upon the whole surface of the globe – the chosen city of the Lord, the place in which it pleased Him to dwell. Every one was silent for a while, absorbed in the deepest contemplation. The object of our pilgrimage was accomplished, and I do not think that anything we saw afterwards during our stay in Jerusalem made a more profound impression on our minds than this first distant view. (Curzon 1983: 192)

Many details of Curzon's account invite comment: the view from the ridge, like that of stout Cortez upon a peak in Darien, is emblematic of Romantic endeavour, a Pisgah-sight for imperialists; 'With one accord' confesses a transcendental sense of submission, augmented by the assumption that the silence of everyone in the party could be spoken for equally, as 'in the deepest contemplation'; in the order of modifiers, 'renowned and sacred', 'the most interesting and venerated', we note the secular value taking syntactic precedence over the devotional. 'The breast of a Christian' rather oddly specifies the faith of one whom the reader might have mistaken for a traveller in search of the glories of the ancient world. And most strikingly, the admission, already, that 'this first distant view' was to make a more profound impression than anything to be seen in Jerusalem itself. That is, of course, very different from earlier pilgrims, such as Felix Fabri and Pietro Casola, from the late Middle Ages, to Lamartine in the early nineteenth century: all are curious, capable of scepticism and declared worldliness, but all share a faith that is to find its realization in particular sites and shrines. Even though we are told that Felix 'had as great an appetite for a view as any Victorian tourist' (Prescott 1954: 79), and although Lamartine is highly appreciative of views, neither would subordinate the proximate to the distant. Lamartine was a Roman Catholic, and Curzon's 'optical subordination' is distinctively Protestant. And, we may add, distinctively imperialistic, always 'on the look-out' for territorial gains in every distance, scanning each horizon for proprietorial potential. Those who bow down, by contrast, submit themselves to the authority of the relic, the shrine, and the land thus sanctified. In a foreign landscape we might suppose that while disinterestedness – Kant's 'necessary condition' for the aesthetic response (Kant 1987: 127 (§29, 267) – would have been fully accordant with the Protestant temperament, it must have taxed the imperialist to the utmost.

Divergent ways of looking have consequences for the ways in which different kinds of pilgrim use and occupy space. Curzon typically values the general view over any specific site, and notices cultural and cultic difference between Protestant pilgrims and those of other confessions:

> It was curious to observe the different effect which our approach to Jerusalem had upon the various persons who composed our party. A Christian pilgrim, who had joined us on the road, fell down upon his knees and kissed the holy ground; two others embraced each other, and congratulated themselves that they had lived to see Jerusalem. As for us Franks, we sat bolt upright upon our horses, and stared and said nothing; whilst around us the more natural children of the East wept for joy ... but we, who consider ourselves civilised and superior beings, repressed our emotions; we were above showing that we participated in the feelings of our barbarous companions.

Curzon goes on, rather disarmingly, to admit that he would like to have followed the example of those companions, but was embarrassed in the presence of other 'Franks':

> As for myself, I would have got off my horse and walked barefooted towards the gate, as some did, if I had dared; but I was in fear of being laughed at for my absurdity, and therefore sat fast in my saddle. At last I blew my nose ... . (Curzon 1983: 192–93)

Curzon's confession is unusual in published recollections; most Protestant pilgrims seem to have been coerced, by the shared dignity of their superiority, into maintaining the appearance of remaining unmoved. The claim to 'deepest contemplation' ought to suffice as excuse for the absence of surface-effects or affects. However profound the impression received by Curzon, he yet confesses the wish for a superficial (and manifest) act of devotion. Yet such an act needs to be undertaken, and in humility. A humble heart is much to be desired, but the posture of a Protestant should be at all times upright: an imperialist ought not to prostrate himself in the presence of 'others', nor publish abroad an act of submission, no matter how transcendent its object.

Over one hundred years later, Curzon's confession still rankles on the Protestant conscience, as acknowledged by Hilda Prescott's account of her fifteenth-century travellers:

> The pilgrims did what pilgrims before and since have done, those, that is to say, who are not inhibited by the Protestant or Victorian shyness which, at the same place, kept Robert Curzon uneasy and self-conscious in his saddle. They dismounted and knelt in the road. (Prescott 1954: 114)

The difference in attitude could lead to practical conflicts over the use of space. One might have thought that the solution was obvious: Protestants could stay on the outskirts, admiring the view, while the others would enter and stay inside the city itself. The others, however, had a way of spoiling the view. As the number of Protestant pilgrims increased, so Curzon's unease would be transformed into something more self-assured, and would manifest itself in a sense of superiority. Curzon's is the most celebrated and cited of early accounts. William Jowett's *Christian Researches in Syria and the Holy Land* had appeared in 1825, and even at this date the same points are made, even more forcefully. Jowett, however, was not in any sense a pilgrim, but had been sent out to the Holy Land as a representative of the Church Missionary Society 'to investigate the prospects and to design an infiltration strategy.' (Hummel 1995: 5) His ideas are not far from those of landscape improvers whose gaze, from the terrace, would sweep cottages and whole villages out of the way to enhance a view of the English countryside. At the Holy Sepulchre, Jowett could not kneel with the other pilgrims; he found distracting not only their demonstrative piety, but the buildings themselves, even the churches:

> Our singularity, no doubt, was remarked by them, as we remained standing; but while we have no desire to offend their feelings, we have also no objection to their knowing that Protestants regard these

ceremonies, as being vain in the sight of God, and detrimental to the simplicity of the Gospel. I felt, moreover, that it would be difficult for me to rise in this place to the spirit of devotion. The fulsome pageantry of the scene must be first removed: the ground of Mount Calvary, now encumbered with convents, churches, and houses and disguised by splendid altars, gaudy pictures, and questionable reliques, must be cleared. (Hummel 1995: 22)

When, within a few years, Protestants themselves became pilgrims, it was a landscape that they came to see. Not surprisingly their eyes were most pleased by sights of vacancy, of desert and ruin, and of high places, the Mount of Olives and Mount Tabor, and the uninterrupted vista across the Sea of Galilee:

The Sea of Galilee was one of the Protestants' favourite spots, not only because it was here that the teaching and preaching of Christ mostly took place, but also because the sites were the landscapes themselves and not buried inside churches and encumbered with encrusted icons ... . Once the ruins of Capernaum were discovered, that also was a place beloved because it was not monumentalized and the site remained 'pure'. (Ibid.: 15–6)

This may be confirmed by the description of Caesarea in Thomas Cook's *Help-Book* of 1870: 'Here now is absolute solitariness. Mr. Gadsby says: "There is not now in Caesarea a single human being." How affecting to think of the extreme contrast of its former greatness and present desolation.' (Burns 1870: 64) Purity and solitude are certainly conducive to Protestant devotion; they may also have had their attractions for territorial prospectors.

Of all the sights and sites of the Holy Land, none was more contaminated than the Holy Sepulchre. Protestants habitually compared the Holy Sepulchre to the Temple from which Christ had expelled the moneylenders. As the Revd. Jabez Burns comments: 'Nothing can possibly be more opposed to the simplicity of Christ than the gorgeous decorations, costly shrines, and superstitious ceremonies of the "Church of the Holy Sepulchre".'(Burns 1870: 83) However, as the English were, for once, in no position to take charge, purify and improve, they cast doubt on the authenticity of its location, and proposed a more fitting alternative, soon to be known as the 'Garden Tomb' on 'Gordon's Calvary'. (Gordon 1884: 1–3) The proposed alternative quickly became popular with Protestants: 'There it was possible to "see" the biblical story coming alive, where no foreign religious element polluted the site with superstitious nonsense. Even today the site is popular among the Evangelical Christians for the same reasons.' (Hummel 1995: 21) In this passage the modern commentators confess their Protestantism: taking as axiomatic the 'simplicity' of Christianity, they collude, to exorbitant lexical effect, in labelling what is not simple as 'foreign'. Protestant pilgrims were constantly lamenting the superstitions and idolatry of others, and proclaiming their own concern for historical veracity; yet, in the Garden Tomb, they chose the aesthetic over the truthful, as John Kelman in *The Holy Land* (1904) hinted:

> It would indeed be a striking thing, if after all the idolatry of sites which the vision of St. Helena started, the real hill and garden where the world's greatest tragedy was enacted should have gone past Roman and Greek worshippers both, and to have been committed to the hands of the simple Protestants. (Hummel 1995: 21)

To English Protestants may thus be ascribed a charge of 'aesthetic idolatry', a preference for sites of solitude and prospects of beauty over those determined by topographical and historical exactitude.

That this was not entirely unconscious is suggested by the implicit desire to claim that Jesus himself was something of a Romantic wanderer; that He, if He were alive today, would choose those spots within the vicinity of Jerusalem best suited to the Protestant temperament. James Cuthbertson, a Wesleyan minister and author of *Sacred and Historic Lands* (1855), writes of the view of Galilee from the outskirts of Nazareth: 'I could not help thinking of more sacred eyes which had looked upon these sights and ranged these landscapes.' (Hummel 1995: 17) Early in the twentieth century Sir Frederick Treves, in *The Land that is Desolate: An Account of a Tour in Palestine* (1913), again ascribed to Jesus the Protestant optic and an enthusiasm for walking: 'This is the country that was transversed by the feet of Christ. This is the very view that, in every dip and knoll, was familiar to His eyes.' (Hummel 1995: 24–5)

The anthropologist Glenn Bowman explains that

> the Protestant desire to have an unmediated relation to the Bible means that a holy place covered over with Orthodox or Catholic churches is, in effect, a site which commemorates institutional domination rather than the truth which that institution has usurped and distorted ... . Consequently, Protestants tend to want to witness Christ himself and not his putative agents, and prefer to frequent places, such as the area around the Sea of Galilee or the Garden Tomb in Jerusalem where they can imagine Christ *in situ.* (Bowman 1991: 116)

If one dislikes mediation, it is of course somewhat illogical to visit the Holy Land at all. In order to resolve or occlude the contradiction, Jesus is to be presented as a fellow-seeker after the unmediated Divine, as if He were not the object of the pilgrimage, but as if He were himself merely the first and chief of pilgrims.

This provides the context for those romantic landscape descriptions that occupy so many pages of nineteenth-century lives of Jesus, including that of Ernest Renan; and for those depictions of the life of Jesus that illustrate so many Protestant Bibles. The anachronistic assumption is that Jesus would somehow have acquired an optical sense trained by perspective in the appreciation of landscape art, and a Kantian spirituality attuned to the challenge of the sublime. Furthermore, in quest of landscapes that would inspire, it was supposed that Jesus would have developed the walking habits of a Wordsworth.

William Hazlitt (1778–1830) was a contemporary of Reginald Heber. His essay, 'On Going a Journey' of *c.*1820 exemplifies and renders thematic the difference between pilgrimage and what would later be called 'rambling' (Parker 1994: 83–86), a difference measured in the history of the word 'saunter' from its origins: 'going à la Sainte Terre', or rather, going nowhere in particular while pretending to be on pilgrimage, as Thoreau explains in the opening of his great essay of 1862, 'Walking'. (Wallace 1993: 180) Hazlitt liked to walk on his own, while carrying a book to read when he had reached his destination. On his twentieth birthday, 10 April 1798, he concluded his day's walking with a reading in Rousseau's *Nouvelle Héloise* of the passage in which St Preux describes the Vaud from the heights of the Jura. Hazlitt is reading this 'sublime' passage by design and with forethought, for he is in Llangollen, having walked along the valley of the Dee 'which opens like an amphitheatre, broad, barren hills rising in majestic state on either side'. The view had prompted him, while still walking, to cite from memory some lines of Coleridge. Hazlitt finds within, however, words which add sublimity to outward sight, and reinscribes the pilgrimage in the sauntering: 'But besides the prospect which opened beneath my feet, another also opened to my inward sight, a heavenly vision, on which were written ... these four words, LIBERTY, GENIUS, LOVE, VIRTUE. ...' (Hazlitt 1930: 78) That heavenly vision or inward sight is one that Protestant pilgrims crave, even when their eyes are looking on the Holy Land.

In the late fourth century, less than a hundred years after the Empress Helena had established the pattern and fashion of pilgrimage, Jerome and Gregory of Nyssa both wrote letters advising ascetics not to undertake the pilgrimage to the Holy Land. Their objections quickly achieved axiomatic status: what is the point of the Church, of its universal call and reach, of the multiplicity of its sacred places and liturgies, if a special status is to be given to one particular place? Jerome protests that monks who follow the ascetic life will be admitted to Paradise whether or not they have visited Jerusalem. Origen, the most allegorical of Christian theologians, insisted that God was to be worshipped everywhere, and that to confer distinction on the Holy Land was to revert from a universal to a local religion. It has been argued (Schmemann 1966: 125–31) that secularization began when one region was named 'the Holy Land': so much for the sanctity of elsewhere.

No nineteenth-century Protestant pilgrim from Britain would have been unaware of Jerome's insistence, fifteen hundred years earlier, that 'Heaven is open equally to those in Britain as to those in Jerusalem'. Contemporaneous with Protestant pilgrimages to the Holy Land we find as a common theme of English verse – not of the highest order – an affirmation of Jerome's view. There are few poems about pilgrimages to the Holy Land – the most important of which we are soon to note – but a

number that, as it were, apologise for staying at home. Francis
Thompson's 'In No Strange Land' takes the 'inward vision' as validating
wherever one happens to be: so one might be granted a vision of 'Jacob's
ladder / Pitched betwixt Heaven and Charing Cross' – 'And lo, Christ
walking on the water, / Not of Gennesareth, but Thames!' (Methuen 1921:
219). E.H. Young in his 'Christmas' (1914) contrasts his own willingness
to die for his friends and neighbours on the Marlborough Downs with the
willingness of Jesus 'to die for men he never knew'. But the final stanza
qualifies such self-deprecation with a bathetic reduction of Christ's
compassion to the local sympathies of a minor late Romantic poet:

> And yet, I think, at Golgotha,
>   as Jesus' eyes were closed in death,
> they saw with love most passionate
>   the village street at Nazareth.   (Methuen 1921: 247)

Rather as pilgrims in the Holy Land must cultivate their inward vision in
order not to see the vulgar crowds, so Jesus, by closing his eyes in death,
shutting out the sight of soldiers and the mob, can enjoy the 'inward
vision' of the places of childhood memories. These are poems
symptomatic of the tensions felt in visiting the Holy Land, or simply in
thinking about Jesus as located in a space assimilated to the aesthetics of
landscape.

Jerome was not the only saint to speak against the rise of pilgrimages.
Gregory of Nyssa asks what function the altar has in each and every
church, if it is somehow less of a site of the Divine Presence than is
Jerusalem. (Hunt 1982: 91–92) In advancing this objection, the cult of
relics has an important function in diminishing the centripetal attractions
of Jerusalem. As Jesus had told his disciples to go out into all the world
and preach the gospel to every creature (Mark 16: 15), so pilgrims were
encouraged to take home with them relics, to disperse through 'all the
world' fragments of the Holy Land. Altars, as far as is known, had been
consecrated simply by the performance of a rite; sometime between the
fifth and ninth centuries, it became established that every altar should be
covered by the antimension, a cloth into which a relic is sown. The
history of this development is obscure, but it is surely related to the need

for the dispersed and multiple altars of Christendom to 'keep up with' and even participate in the growing prestige of the Holy Land.

Jerome himself conceded some of the advantages of seeing 'by the evidence of my own eyes' the places heard about through the Bible. (Hunt 1982: 100) In this respect, Jerome was not unlike many of the Protestant pilgrims for whom the Gospel 'came alive' through visiting the locations of its setting. Typical is J.M.P. Otts whose book of 1893 is entitled with astounding presumption: *The Fifth Gospel: The Land where Jesus Lived*. Acres of landscape are explicitly set against acres of print: 'Thus the well-informed and observant traveler in the land of the Bible will find more to confirm its truth and unfold its meaning while journeying through the land where Jesus lived, than he could ever gather from whole acres of printed evidences of Christianity.' (Hummel 1995: 31) Somewhat paradoxically, Jerome allowed pilgrimages to the Holy Land as a way of encouraging and defending the cult of relics. Yet devout eyes should be able to derive as much from relics as from a visit to the Holy Land itself: both should be seen with inward vision; both should serve as clues to a vision beyond the sensory. Indeed, properly understood, the Holy Land should itself be treated as a relic (albeit on a vast and nonportable scale), rather than as the source and origin of relics. Thus a fragment of wood is not to be thought holy because it comes from the Holy Land; the Holy Land itself is holy only because it has been, like a portable relic, in contact with the Divine. And the specific place and time of Christ's incarnation is not a limitation for the Holy Spirit, which may inspire one's vision of the Dee or the Jordan, or the Thames.

Furthermore, the inward vision that in the nineteenth century would be related to the sublime and to broad vistas and sweeping prospects, is for Jerome appropriate specifically to small things. E.D. Hunt has pointed out the importance of the visual in the defence and propagation of relics by Jerome and others. Writing in 403 to Sulpicius Severus, Paulinus of Nola encloses a fragment of the cross: 'All that Severus will see with his naked eye is a few scraps of wood; but this is only a stimulus to the wider lens of his "interior eyesight" [*interna acies*] which will summon up a picture ... "with his interior eyesight he will see the whole meaning of the Cross in this tiny fragment."' (Hunt 1982: 132) Interior eyesight, the eyes of faith, the inward vision: these terms name the spiritual faculty which all Christians can cultivate, whether or not they visit the Holy Land. But in the nineteenth century, 'inner vision' is what Protestant pilgrims need, especially when they might be distracted by the outward sights of the Holy Land: inner vision is what protects the eyes from the obtrusive particulars of shrines and crowds. The inner vision can restore the distant view.

No Protestant in the nineteenth century would have questioned the universal availability of the Sublime, emanating indifferently from the Jordan or the Dee. The Sublime is, briefly, the acknowledgement of an 'external immeasurable' that corresponds to the immeasurability of inward vision. The discourse of the 'landscape sublime' from the mid-eighteenth century seems to respond to Petrarch's account of his ascent of Mont Ventoux, at the summit of which he reads Augustine, who tells him that the mind is as vast and unfathomable as any mountain or ocean: 'I myself cannot grasp the totality of what I am'. (cited in Lock 1999: 187–89) The sublime is not singular: it is constituted by the parity of inward and outward vision. The importance of that correspondence could not be more clearly indicated than by Hazlitt's 'vision of words': the landscape calls forth words, not as heard but as seen, as if lettered across the view. Something similar should, of course, occur to every pilgrim in the Holy Land, whose outward sight will call forth in inward vision the words of remembered prayers and scriptural passages.

The concept of the Sublime cannot be detached from Protestantism: God is that which can be thought of as the excess of intellection over sense. God's divinity and numinousness will be stressed, his incarnation, his participation in the material sensory world, diminished. Nor can the Sublime be thought of apart from the development of pictorial perspective. The horizon is the figure of sensory limit, beyond which lies the invisible, immeasurable, unattainable, the outward cause of sublimity. The vanishing-point is the crux, the chiastic node, signalling a beyond that can never be reached. It is futile to approach close to a picture in which there is a vanishing-point: the vanishing-point will determine the proper distance from which the painting is to be viewed. A picture that has no horizon, and no vanishing-point, such as the icon in the Orthodox tradition, has no capacity to keep the spectator at a distance. Indeed, the devout spectator is drawn so close as to participate in the space of the icon, by bowing down, by kissing (Lock 1997).

Protestant pilgrims go in search of landscapes in which they can experience the Sublime, and in which they can imagine Jesus, not as Christ, one of the Holy Trinity, but as a man, Himself a lone seeker after the sublime. The Holy Land acquires prestige among Protestants in the mid-nineteenth century because it contains those landscapes in which Jesus, gazing over valleys and hills towards the distant horizon, would have experienced the Sublime.

The Protestant task is always to return to that first simplicity which so exactly matches the Protestant's own. The plainness of the landscape is itself held up as evidence of the truth of Protestantism. Had a more luscious or spectacular land been chosen for the home of Jesus, the religion that He established might with more justification have been resplendent. However, in the words of Sir Frederick Treves:

> It was in this plain and unassuming country that the religion of Christ was taught. It was taught in the simplest language, in words that a child could understand, and by means of illustrations drawn from the lowliest of subjects. There was in the teaching no stilted ritual, no gorgeous ceremony, no foreshadowing of the princely prelate or the chanting priest. It was a religion associated with such sounds as the splash of a fisherman's net in the lake, the patter of sheep, the call of the shepherd, the tramp of the sower across the fields. (Hummel 1995: 25)

This landscape is not only plain; it is almost English. From the proper aesthetic distance, all shepherds and fishermen, of whatever culture or time or place, appear much the same. And it is by the 'optics of assimilation' that Protestant pilgrims cultivate the distant prospect, for at a distance all things tend to look alike. The pagan's attention to wood and stone, and the Orthodox pilgrim's kissing of icons and relics, must strike such perspectival viewers as myopic, as well as barbaric: the heathen in his *blindness*. Another of Hazlitt's essays, of *c.*1821, is entitled 'Why Distant Objects Please'. After the celebration of the freedom of the mind and of the fancy in the sight of 'misty mountain-tops,' Hazlitt speaks of disillusionment:

> Passion is lord of infinite space, and distant objects please because they border on its confines and are moulded by its touch. When I was a boy,

I lived within sight of a range of lofty hills, whose blue tops blending with the setting sun had often tempted my longing eyes and wandering feet. At last I put my project in execution, and on a nearer approach, instead of glimmering air woven into fantastic shapes, found them huge lumpish heaps of discoloured earth. (Hazlitt 1930: 127–28)

Too close a scrutiny of the Holy Landscape might reveal the shepherds and fishermen to be of alien, Semitic cast; to come close to the holy sites is to see all the alien and alienating excrescences of superstition and, of course, the other pilgrims, themselves not alienated but contiguous with their own idea of sanctity. One should (in Protestant phrase) keep one's distance.

For the nineteenth century, a sense of distance was inseparable from reason: perspectival distance goes with cognitive detachment. The concepts of logos and reason underwrite those of ratio, proportion and perspective. The sublime is, for Kant, what exceeds our grasp of ratio, insofar as proportion is demonstrable to the senses. Kant's theory of the sublime is a reprise of Anselm's proof of the existence of God – that God must exist as the ground of our capacity to posit His existence. According to Anselm: 'that than which nothing greater can be thought cannot be in the intellect alone ... Therefore, beyond doubt, something than which nothing greater can be thought exists in intellect and also in reality. And this art Thou, o Lord.' (Tillich 1968: 162–63) According to Kant: 'Nothing that can be the object of the senses is to be called sublime ... Our imagination strives to progress towards infinity, while our reason demands absolute totality. This inadequacy [of reason] itself is the arousal within us of the feeling that we have within us a supersensible power'. And Kant clinches his argument (and discloses his allusion to Anselm) thus: '*Sublime is what even to be able to think proves that the mind has a power surpassing any power of sense.*' (Kant 1987: 106 [§25: 250])

That the Sublime is a displacement of the theological is clear. Comparison between groups of pilgrims may help to show where the Sublime is lurking, latent, among non-Protestants. Both Bowman (1991) and the Hummels, in their brief but extremely suggestive book (Hummel 1995), have explored the differences between Protestant and other pilgrims, of whom the Hummels focus on the Russian Orthodox. Of the latter, Bowman records his own observation (made in the 1980s) that Orthodox pilgrims are entirely lacking in distance or detachment. They know only of objects to be reached and touched, a shrine, an icon, a relic. Protestants have no such particular objects, because particularity involves proximity, and Protestants wish to have a prospect, and maintain their distance: not only from shrines and relics, but from the unwashed pilgrims of other churches. Orthodox pilgrims treat the Holy Land much as they treat the sacralized spaces of the Orthodox Church or of the domestic icon corner. They show no interest in the view, nor in history:

> I was bemused, while travelling with Orthodox pilgrims, to see that the guides always presented biblical and historical information about holy places ... and that the pilgrims were so uninterested in those details that ... the guides took to keeping the pilgrims confined to the buses until they had finished. ... Once released, the pilgrims would rush impatiently into the churches and proceed around the interiors kissing all the icons without granting any – except perhaps those of Jesus and the Virgin Mary – particular attention. (Bowman 1991: 110)

Bowman makes a number of pertinent observations: that icons depicting events associated with the present site, or relics of that site, received no more attention than any others; that the Russian pilgrims paid special attention rather to icons concerning themselves and their own time. That is to say, the icon of one's own saint (whose name one shares), or the icon of today's feast, or of the saint commemorated on this day. While Protestant pilgrims stress the unprecedented nature of the experience, the uniqueness of the place, Orthodox pilgrims may show particular devotion to an icon whose type they recognise from icons at home. These pilgrims are almost oblivious of space, and are guided by liturgical time. Bowman notes:

> Travels around the holy places are, for the Orthodox, a desirable but unnecessary supplement to their pilgrimage; what the pilgrimage to the Holy Land is about, at heart, is being present in Jerusalem during the holy feasts. It is during these festivals that the significant realism of the holy places comes into play. ... (Bowman 1991: 111)

Where Protestants practise a form of 'aesthetic assimilation', the Orthodox pilgrims practise a 'liturgical assimilation' by which they can subsume difference and novelty within the familiar liturgical cycles and devotional spaces.

We have suggested that the cult of relics was developed, from the time of St Jerome, not to enhance the prestige of the Holy Land as their source, but to encourage an understanding of the Holy Land as itself a relic: that is to say, not holy in itself, but holy as a relic is, by contact or derivation. Bowman suggests that, for the Orthodox, the Holy Land does enjoy a special status, not because it is or contains some essence in itself, but because 'the Holy Land ... is the most realistic icon' (Bowman 1991: 110). And, of course, what the Orthodox do with icons is not to look at them from a pleasing distance, but to kiss them (Lock 1997). This point is made by Gary Vikan, who further argues that the Orthodox pilgrims in the Holy Sepulchre would identify themselves with those followers looking for the body of their Lord: they would become 'iconically one and the same' with the participants in that event whose liturgical celebration is not a commemoration but a sacramental 'making present' (Vikan 1990: 101–6; Hummel 1995: 53).

For the Orthodox pilgrims, then, time is elided, as time is always elided by the liturgical rhythms; for the Protestants, by contrast, their presence in the Holy Land is motivated by the newly discovered significance of history, of archaeology, and of geology: a sense of time as marker and measure of distance and difference. To the Protestants, furthermore, travel is an opportunity for seeing, for viewing prospects, for constituting landscapes as one walks or rides through the countryside; and thereby imagining what it must have been that other eyes had seen, long ago. For the Orthodox, travel is insignificant, as is the space that one traverses: all that matters is that Jerusalem is at the centre, the axle-tree of sacred, cosmic time: the spot of earth from which all creation is sacralized. Protestant pilgrims 'lamented the ease of the rail journey; it was a spiritual loss' (Hummel 1995: 12) brought about by their own advanced technology. Orthodox pilgrims, by contrast, are not recorded as making any complaint about any mode of transport, however alien, that would get them to Jerusalem in time for Holy Week.

The conflict between Protestant and non-Protestant pilgrims is thus not simply one of theology or cultic practice. In the distant prospect of

Protestants, non-Protestants are themselves figured as pagans, bowing down to wooden icons and stony relics; and the holy sites are considered to have been desecrated. The proportions of a prospect must not be distorted, nor should the view to the horizon be interrupted. Together, the shrines and the worshippers made the prospect unpleasing; they obstructed the sight-lines, and spoilt the view. Every prospect might be pleasing, if only the pagans, together with their wooden and stone idols, could be cleared away. Yet, of course, what Burke and Kant would identify as the Sublime can be posed as latent in the icons of the Orthodox, of which, in their defence, it is said that one worships not that which is accessible to the senses (mere wood or pigment), but the 'prototype', Christ, His mother or a saint. Not 'beyond' in the manner of perspective, beyond the vanishing-point, or over the horizon, but within the iconic space, constituted by what has been termed 'inverse perspective'.

Our argument is that viewing is not normative, but is historically and ideologically conditioned. The absence of landscape description in earlier pilgrims, which has vexed a number of scholars, is not a problem once it is accepted that the 'landscape' was simply not seen by them. Such recent works as those of Campbell (1991) and Leyerle (1996) seem only among the most sophisticated attempts to answer an erroneously-posed question. Nor should we be surprised that the Protestant optic which drew English travellers to the Holy Land in the nineteenth century is also the optic through which scholars today look at the Holy Land and its pilgrims throughout the centuries.

The longest and most imposing of all literary works to emerge from nineteenth-century Protestant pilgrimages to the Holy Land must be Herman Melville's *Clarel*, published in 1876, drawn from his journey to Europe and the Levant from October 1856 to May 1857. A poem of nearly 18,000 lines, *Clarel* is subtitled, intriguingly, 'A Poem and Pilgrimage in the Holy Land'. The two odd words here are 'and' and 'in', where we would expect 'A poem of a pilgrimage to the Holy Land.' That the poem is itself a pilgrimage is, however, an idea that no reader who endures could resist for long. It is an arduous journey, and one that seems to go nowhere in particular, for it begins in Jerusalem, and ends in a curious criss-crossing of birth and death, in Bethlehem during Holy Week. All that we have noted in the preference of Protestant pilgrims for distant prospects is summed in one couplet in the very first canto:

> Romance of mountains! But in end
> What change the near approach could lend.
> (Melville 1991: I.1.48)

Just as Hazlitt was disappointed to find that his blue remembered hills were mere lumpish heaps, so Melville records in his travel journal that he saw, when close, not a pastoral landscape, which from a distance had resembled England, but a desolation: 'the diabolical landscapes [of a] great part of Judea must have suggested to the Jewish prophets, their ghastly theology' (Melville 1955: 151). The change of the near approach is to realize the hills as even worse than lumpish heaps, nothing but stones:

> In divers way which vary it
> Stones mention find in hallowed Writ:
> Stones rolled from well-mouths, altar stones,
> Idols of stone, memorial ones,
> Sling-stones, stone tables ...
>
> Attesting here the Holy Writ –
> In brook, in glen, by tomb and town
> In natural way avouching it –
> Behold the stones! And never one
> A lichen greens; and, turns them o'er –
> No worm – no life; but, all the more,
> Good witnesses.
> (Melville, 1991: 2.10.1–33)

The stones are witnesses, not as though the stones themselves might cry out, but mute external and sensory witnesses to the textual frequency of stones in Scripture. Moreover, Clarel's romantic view of the mountains would seem to benefit from hindsight and the cumulative attitudes of travellers; in his *Journal* Melville disdains even the view: 'On way to

Bethelam saw Jerusalem from distance – unless knew it, could not have recognized it – looked exactly like arid rocks.' (Melville 1951: 139) And Rolfe, Clarel's closest companion on the pilgrimage, makes the characteristically Protestant comment:

> 'Strange! of the sacred places here,
> And all through Palestine indeed,
> Not one we Protestants hold dear
> Enough to tend and care for.'
> (Melville 1991: 4.7.47–50)

To which a Lutheran priest responds that, long before Luther had at once discouraged pilgrimages and established Protestantism, the sites were already assigned:

> 'These legend-precincts high and low
> In custody already were
> Of Greek and Latin, who retain.
> So even did we wish to be
> Shrine-keepers here and share the fee –
> No sites for Protestants remain.'
> (Melville 1991: 4.7.80–5)

General Gordon had not yet proposed the alternative 'Garden Tomb'. Clarel's fellow-pilgrim, Ungar, described as a 'wandering Ishmael,' goes outside after compline and feels within himself an atavistic impulse to worship the stars, and through them, their Creator, as Job (9:8–9) had worshipped God 'which alone spreadeth out the heavens ... Which maketh ... the chambers of the south':

> 'How might his hand not go to mouth
> In kiss adoring ye, bright zones?
> Look up: the age, the age forget –
> There's something to look up to yet!'
> (Melville 1991: 4.7.97–100)

The sublime option is one that can hardly be resisted for those who ignore what's close, or resent it as already possessed, already taken care of, and cultivate the numinous in the distance. Yet we note that even when kissing is invoked, it is a kiss of what is beyond reach, an abstract kiss, very different from that in which lips come in contact with wood and stone.

Ungar's kiss is uncannily close to that of Gerard Manley Hopkins in the fifth stanza of 'The Wreck of the Deutschland', written in the very same year that saw *Clarel* published, 1876:

> I kiss my hand
> To the stars, lovely-asunder
> Starlight, wafting him out of it; and
> Glow, glory in thunder;
> Kiss my hand to the dappled-with-damson west ... .

These are distant kisses, and Hopkins as a convert to Roman Catholicism would, of course, find nothing tasteless or rebarbative in oscular veneration and prostration. But the gesture of a kiss towards the horizon, the starlight, the vanishing-point, is symptomatic of the economy of tension between seeing and touching which we have attempted to trace. (And in Hopkins, of course, symptomatic of the tension between his faith and his Romantic aesthetic.)

Seeing into the distance – admiring the prospect – comes at a cost: of not seeing what's close at hand; or rather, of *only* seeing it. The Sublime is taken as 'evidence not seen' of what is beyond seeing. And it is the Sublime that excludes an equal and opposite faith in the 'evidence not seen' in what is near at hand. Those who have no perspectival optic can see within wood or stone the transcendence that calls on them to bow down in veneration. Those who find the prospect pleasing will, by contrast, see in wood and stone only wood, only stone.

The most appropriate response to the Protestant optic comes from no Christian source but – oddly enough, given the imbrications of Protestantism and neo-Platonism – from Plotinus's follower and assistant, and somewhat dissentient biographer, Porphyry:

It is no wonder that those who are complete ignoramuses regard statues as mere wood and stone, just as those who are ignorant of letters look upon inscribed markers as nothing more than stones or upon writing tablets as nothing more than pieces of wood or upon books as nothing more than papyrus woven together. (Finney 1994: 52)

Reginald Heber should have attended to Porphyry. For it is sheer ignorance to see statues as 'mere wood and stone', and arrogance to suppose that veneration of such statues or icons is mere superstition. The heathen's 'blindness' is another way of seeing, a way that depends not on distance but on proximity, one that involves a recognition of that which is depicted. Recognition, that dramatic moment of *anagnorisis* that precipitates *proskinesis*, the act of veneration, the bowing down, the kiss: recognition is the end and aim of pilgrimage. The rest is sightseeing. And the discourse of modernity favours those who take the longer view. In a poem written 'At sea, June 16, 1833', 'The Pillar of the Cloud', that would become (as 'Lead, kindly light') a hymn as famous in its way as Heber's, J.H. Newman knows what is at stake in the development of human optics. And he holds with precision his rejection of the view, of the prospect of modernity:

> I do not ask to see
> The distant scene, – one step enough for me.
> (*English Hymnal* 1933: 570 (no. 425))

References

Bowman, G. (1991) 'Christian ideology and the image of a holy land: The place of Jerusalem pilgrimage in the various Christianities', in J. Eade and M. Sallnow (eds) *Contesting the Sacred: The Anthropology of Christian Pilgrimage.* London: Routledge, pp. 98–121.

Burns, Revd. J., D.D. and Thomas Cook, (1870) *Help-Book for Travellers to the East.* London: Cook's.

Campbell, M.B. (1991) '"The Object of One's Gaze": Landscape, Writing, and Early Medieval Pilgrimage', in S. Westrem (ed.) *Discovering New Worlds: Essays on Medieval Exploration and Imagination*. New York: Garland, pp. 3–15.

Curzon, R. (1983) *Visits to Monasteries in the Levant* [1849] London: Century.

Daniel, G. (1950) *A Hundred Years of Archaeology*. London: Duckworth.

Elliott-Binns, L.E. (1956) *English Thought 1860–1900: The Theological Aspect*. London: Longman.

English Hymnal with Tunes (1933). Oxford: Oxford University Press.

Finney, P. (1994), *The Invisible God: The Earliest Christians on Art*. New York: Oxford University Press.

Gordon, C.G. (1884) *Reflections in Palestine 1883*. London: Macmillan.

Hazlitt, W. (1930) *Selected Essays of William Hazlitt*, ed. G. Keynes. London: Nonesuch.

Hummel, R. and Hummel, T. (1995) *Patterns of the Sacred: English Protestant and Russian Orthodox Pilgrims of the Nineteenth Century*. London: Scorpion Cavendish (with the Swedish Christian Study Centre, Jerusalem).

Hunt, E.D., (1982) *Holy Land Pilgrimage in the Late Roman Empire AD 312–460*. Oxford: Clarendon Press.

Hussey, C. (1967) *The Picturesque: Studies in a Point of View* [1927] London: Cass.

Kant, I. (1987) *Critique of Judgment*, trans W.S. Pluhar. Indianapolis: Hackett.

Leyerle, B. (1996) 'Landscape as Cartography in Early Christian Pilgrim Narratives', *Journal of the American Academy of Religion* 64: 119–43.

Lock, C. (1997) 'Iconic Space and the Materiality of the Sign', *Religion and the Arts* 1(4): 6–22.

—— (1999) 'Michel de Certeau: Walking the *via negativa*', *Paragraph* 22(2): 184–98.

Melville, H. (1955) *Journal of a Visit to Europe and the Levant*, ed. H.C. Horsford. Princeton University Press.

—— (1991) *Clarel: A Poem and Pilgrimage in the Holy Land* (Evanston, I.L.: Northwestern University Press.

Methuen, A. (ed.) (1921) *An Anthology of Modern Verse*. London: Methuen.

Parker, D. (1994) 'Rambling Dickensians', in P. Dávidházi and J. Karafiáth (eds) *Literature and its Cults*. Budapest: Argumentum, pp. 83–96.

Prescott, H.F.M. (1954) *Jerusalem Journey: Pilgrimage to the Holy Land in the Fifteenth Century*. London: Eyre & Spottiswoode.

Schmemann, A. (1966) *Introduction to Liturgical Theology*, trans. A.E. Moorhouse. Crestwood, NY: St Vladimir's Seminary Press.

Tillich, P. (1968) *A History of Christian Thought*. New York: Simon & Schuster.

Vikan, G. (1990) 'Pilgrims in Magi's Clothing: The Impact of Mimesis on Early Byzantine Pilgrimage Art', in R. Ousterhout (ed) *The Blessings of Pilgrimage*, Urbana, IL.: The University of Illinois Press, pp. 97–107.

Wallace, A.D. (1993) *Walking, Literature, and English Culture: The Origins and Uses of Peripatetic in the Nineteenth Century*. Oxford: Clarendon Press.

Postcards from the Edge of History: Narrative and the Sacralisation of Mormon Historical Sites

Hildi J. Mitchell
University of Sussex

Since the 1980s, the anthropology of pilgrimage has moved away from its traditional focus on the exoticisms of non-Christian pilgrimage (e.g. Karve 1962; Rabinow 1975; Gold 1988) towards an analysis of pilgrimage in more familiar settings (e.g. Coleman and Elsner 1998). Partly as a result of this shift of ethnographic focus, recent anthropology of pilgrimage has also been marked by a shift of emphasis from a broadly structuralist approach informed by the influential work of Victor Turner (e.g. Turner and Turner 1978) towards a concern with the heterogeneity of the pilgrimage experience. Eade and Sallnow, for example, in the introduction to their recently reprinted *Contesting the Sacred: The Anthropology of Christian Pilgrimage*, urge us not only to recognise that pilgrimage is

> above all an arena for competing religious and secular discourses, for the official co-optation and the non-official recovery of religious meaning, for conflict between orthodoxies, sects, and confessional groups, for drives towards consensus and communitas, *and* for counter-movements towards separateness and division (Eade and Sallnow 2000: 2)

but also to 'deconstruct the very category of "pilgrimage" into historically and culturally specific behaviours and meanings'. While this does not necessarily mean that they have adopted a postmodernist approach, disregarding structure completely (see Coleman 2001: 29), it has led, perhaps rightly, as an antidote to previous work, to an overemphasis on the role of individual innovation in the pilgrimage experience (e.g. Coleman and Elsner 1998). While it would be wrong to suggest that work such as Coleman's fails to understand the constraints upon individual pilgrims, it does privilege the heterogeneity of pilgrimage sites and experiences, rather than the ways in which structures serve to successfully homogenise and control pilgrimage and related religious experiences.

One reason that the study of Mormon pilgrimage does not fit easily into the agenda outlined by Eade and Sallnow is because of the ways in which Mormon history is experienced in a successfully homogenised manner. Primarily, this is a result of the way in which history works in important ways as theology for Mormons. Davies (1989: 170 and 2000: 11) argues that history often plays within Mormonism the role occupied in other religions by theology, which fits Troeltsch's categorisation of sects who have, rather than a theology, a 'living mythos' (Davies 2000: 11). Members who subscribe to the Mormon way of life – the 'strict ethic', the 'living mythos' and the 'passionate hope for the future', to use Troeltsch's terms (1931: 996) – necessarily align themselves with a particular version of Mormon history, as well as a canon of beliefs and doctrines. The use of proselytising missionaries as guides in visitors centres is one obvious example of this theology-as-history, but it goes much further, including the mentioning of particular sites on the Mormon landscape in modern Mormon scripture. The *Doctrine and Covenants*, which documents the early history of the Mormon Church, is revered as scripture, and it contains mention, for example, of Mormon settlements in Nauvoo, Illinois, and Far West, Missouri. It also documents reported visitations by Christ and other heavenly beings to named places in America. The lessons and scriptural messages of this book come in the form of revelations allegedly given to Joseph Smith as a response to the struggles of the early Latter-day Saints, thus tying theological principles closely to historical events (see Mitchell 2001). The Church thus controls the dissemination and interpretation of history through claiming it as theology. All Mormons receive instruction in reading the *Doctrine and Covenants*, at Sunday School and other scripture study classes (e.g. 'Seminary' and 'Institute'[1]) but the historical narrative is subsumed under theological instruction, as Sunday School teachers throughout the world follow a centrally coordinated guideline of lesson plans. It is no coincidence though, that, where individuals do have conflict with the Church, these conflicts often coalesce around the issue of history. It is precisely because history is for most purposes theology that its study 'can easily be read as an exercise in orthodoxy or heresy' (Davies 2000: 11). Some of my non-mainstream informants related how they were angry with the Church for 'hiding' aspects of their past – for example, the extent to which polygamy was practised after it was publicly renounced by the Church, or the strength of Joseph Smith's interests in Freemasonry (see e.g. Buerger 1994) – and this perceived hypocrisy was a key factor in their disillusionment with the Church. Liberal Mormon-interest publications, such as *Sunstone* and *Dialogue: A Journal of Mormon Thought*, carry many features on history and historical controversy,[2] which would not be voiced in any Sunday School lesson or Sacrament Meeting.

Eade and Sallnow have been criticised for introducing a person/place/text triad as an analytical tool for the study of Christian pilgrimage, and then failing to really develop it. Indeed, it has not been taken up elsewhere either (Coleman and Elsner 1995: 202). This is perhaps explained in part by the recent aim of moving away from Turnerian and structural models. As Eade admits in the introduction to the new edition of *Contesting the Sacred*, 'in our enthusiasm for contestation we overstated our deconstruction of pilgrimage as both a category and a structure' (Eade 2000: xiv).

The general mood has also been to consider a perceived increased interest in the sacred landscape in general, rather than organised religion. As it is recognised that: 'for some pilgrims, the journey to a Christian shrine becomes a highly individual, internalised quest for meanings, beyond the boundaries of belief and practice (ibid.: xvi–xvii), the role of particular religious institutions and churches in maintaining authorised meanings has received less attention. Such an approach does not do justice to the nature of a religion such as Mormonism, where corporate control is paramount, and where branded religiohistorical experience is part of the problem of homogeneity, not individual creativity.

This article, which examines the apparently homogenous experiences of Mormon[3] travel in the U.S.A., moves away from the model of contestation and 'pick and mix' spirituality to reexamine the structural aspects of a specific religion, and in particular, to reexplore the person/place/text triad offered by Eade and Sallnow. To look at a religion such as Mormonism without recognising the immense influence of its organisational and hierarchical structures is a mistake. Mormonism does not allow for a 'pick and mix' spirituality. This analysis is not purely structural though, indeed one of the broader aims of this work is to show *how* these structures become embodied and thus powerful (see Mitchell 2001). Moreover, Mormon pilgrimage *does* challenge the secular/religious distinction, and thus does critique the category of 'pilgrimage' as Eade and Sallnow called for us to do (1991). Just as Mormon sacred travel replicates wider structures of Mormon religiosity, so their travel also replicates wider patterns of secular travel and tourism.

Eade and Sallnow introduce the idea of person/place/text in an attempt to provide a framework for the task of interrogating the specificities of individual sites or events of Christian Pilgrimage against a background of 'ever more vacuous' generalisations generated by the perspective of grand narrative (2000: 9). Noting that the very basis of pilgrimage is the concept of the 'holy place'- a place marked off from the profanity of the world which surrounds it (cf. Eliade 1963) – they argue that such sacred spaces may be conceptualised, generated and used in quite different ways in different contexts (Eade and Sallnow 2000: 6). Lourdes, for example, derives its sacredness from the visitation of the Virgin Mary to Bernadette Soubirous on this site, and this sacredness is continually reaffirmed through the miraculous healing powers associated with the grotto. In the Andes, however, the authors point out, there are two quite distinct concepts of sacred place: one is of the shrine which emanates from the natural landscape, while the other is of the consecration of places through visitations of external divinities (ibid.). Sometimes these two perspectives are reconciled in the notion of the shrines as 'petrified bodies of wandering gods, their power emanating from their still-living bodies' (ibid.).

This link with the body of the sacred person provides Eade and Sallnow with their next component in the triad. The sacred centre can consist not of a sacred place, but a sacred person. In the Sri Lankan material discussed in that volume by Stirrat, for example, the living body of the saint is what gives Christian shrines their power, rather than their physical location (Stirrat 2000). Further, Eade and Sallnow argue, 'If a sacred centre offers the opportunity for direct contact with the divine, then relocating that centre in a human body makes the divine even more accessible and responsive to human needs and aspirations' (2000: 7).

The last strand in this model is where the sacred centre is located not in place or person, but in text. In Bowman's contribution to that volume, we see how Christian pilgrimage to the Holy Land can be understood not merely as an identification with Christ by passing through the places where he walked, preached and performed miracles, but as a journey through a particular text – the biblical account of the life of Jesus (Bowman 2000). It is this third modality of Christian pilgrimage which informs my piece, although the others – place and person – are here also. In one sense it is a demonstration of the textual aspect of pilgrimage. We see, here, for instance, that the holy places of Mormonism, like the holy places of Jerusalem for Bowman's Catholics 'radiate no power as such – it is significant that no miraculous healing qualities are associated with them, nor are penitential practices engaged in to tap their sacredness' (Eade and Sallnow 2000: 9) and that they are 'visited as illustrations of a text that is itself the ultimate source of power' (ibid.). However, as well as demonstrating that, for Mormons, as for many other Christians, the power of the word is paramount (cf. Coleman 2000: 117–42), the article seeks to use this insight to explore *how* the power of text and narrative works in the creation of certain places as sacred sites worthy of a kind of pilgrimage, rather than merely of secular tourism. The insights of authors who argue for attention to be paid to heterogeneity are also invoked here, however. Although the aim is to engage with the important 'structuring structures' (see Bourdieu 1990) of Mormonism, the article recognises the importance of individual engagements with Mormon sites and texts. In fact, the article shows how individually produced narratives of the past and the present combine with the authorised word to structure the interpretation of both history and theology.

Firstly, it is argued that religious sites are made sacred, rather than secular, through the ways in which narratives are used. This is accomplished in a number of ways. Scriptural texts are reproduced as monuments at historical sites, thus (re)inscribing scriptural texts into the landscape (often these places themselves appear in scripture). These are often replicated as photographs or postcards. Sites are officially recognised (cf. the recognition of Catholic saints/miracles, Woodward 1996) by the production of 'branded' literature, including guidebooks, leaflets, trail cards etc. Scriptures are re-incorporated into the experiences of the places through the act of reading scriptures, as well as by general prayer and meditation; these are then re-inscribed into journals, postcards, letters etc. as part of testimonies. Finally, narrative is used to create sacred places through the telling of stories.

The second part of the argument suggests that the ways in which these various texts and narratives are used echo parts of Stromberg's (1993) work on conversion narratives. We have to look at these narratives for what they reveal in terms of structure and how they are used, as well as for their referential value. They are also *doing* things – i.e., making places sacred, converting tellers and hearers, making testimonies stronger. Thus Mormon religious travel replicates Mormon religious experience more generally (Mitchell 2001).

The following sections of the paper make use of a variety of texts, narratives and images given to me by informants and friends to illustrate and develop this argument.

Personal diaries

The restored historic Nauvoo is really beautiful. There are 45 missionaries working here, mostly [retired, married] couples, with some young men and women. They live in some of the restored houses, others are open to the public. The missionaries show you round and explain things. We saw a film in the visitors' centre about the building of Nauvoo and its history. Then we went on a wagon drawn by two big Belgian horses and driven by Elder Sperry [one of the missionaries] from Idaho ...

In the evening we went to a show at the visitors' centre which featured 6 lady missionaries and 6 Elders who sang, acted and danced the history of Nauvoo, including crossing the [Mississippi] river. All their information was taken from journals and historical records. It was very good ...

> Nauvoo is really beautiful and it's very humbling to think of the tremendous sacrifice the saints[4] made as they first built the city and then left it in the space of 7 years. (Kathy, Personal Journal, 1992)

After being expelled from Missouri in 1838, the Mormon pioneers built a new settlement on swampy land in Illinois. This town was named Nauvoo, but it was only a short time before they were on the move again, pushed out further west towards the Salt Lake Valley in Utah. The area of Nauvoo has been extensively restored, as it has been reacquired by both the Church of Jesus Christ of Latter-day Saints (LDS) and the Reorganised Church of Jesus Christ of Latter-Day Saints (RLDS). A leaflet published by the LDS Church on 'Nauvoo the Beautiful' sets out the religious significance of the place for Mormons, giving a brief history of the Church's establishment, before suggesting that Nauvoo also 'provides a window into the past and into the lives of a people who helped settle this nation'. The background to a visit to Nauvoo, then, encompasses several aspects: it is an historic Mormon settlement which in particular stands for the persecution of the early saints; it represents American, rather than simply Mormon, pioneers; and it is dominated by the presence of both the LDS and RLDS Churches. More than that, it is also a 'heritage' experience, as is evident from the accounts of wagon rides and music shows as part of the interpretative armour of the site. The personal journal entries about visiting Nauvoo reflect these things, but in particular ways. Their narratives of these aspects of Nauvoo are coloured by both the historical narrative they have gained from the *Doctrine and Covenants* itself, and from the way this scripture is taught in Church. Further, however, they bear the print of other Mormon narratives, in particular one with which these visitors are more familiar – the testimony.

Kathy's journal entry about her stay in Nauvoo begins, not with any reflection on the 'real' old Nauvoo, but with reference both to the restoration of the site, and to the missionary presence. The apparent primacy of these aspects of her experience of the place reflects a Mormon internalisation of a particular kind of history. Firstly, history is something to be reconstructed for present day 'saints' to learn from. Secondly, the 'reconstruction' (there is little sense here or elsewhere in popular Mormon reflections of the problematic nature of 're-constructing' the past), is something which is done both by the Church (the LDS Church owns many of the Nauvoo buildings) and for a specific theological purpose (hence the use of proselytising missionaries as tour guides). This controlled sacralisation of Nauvoo and other sites follows a pattern set up in Mormon weekly church-going. Members study Church history alongside the study of the Church texts, the Book of Mormon and the *Doctrine and Covenants*, being taught these history lessons on Sundays, by Sunday School teachers, rather than history teachers or scholars. In these lessons, the emphasis is often on the spiritual lessons to be learned from history. For example, a lesson from one of the manuals for the Church's organisation for women, Relief Society, focuses on the importance of learning about Mormon heritage. It states:

> We are a history-making and a history-keeping people. We value our heritage and honor the great vision, faith and courage of the men and women who have struggled and sacrificed to build the kingdom of God on the earth. (*Follow Me*, 1992: 153)

It goes on to say that, 'Learning about the pioneers in our own areas can strengthen our testimonies and increase our desires to serve the Lord' (p.155). Learning about the past, then, is not a pleasure or a duty in itself, but is a tool to increase spirituality in the present. Other lessons in other handbooks give readings of particular historical events, such as the famous story of the plague of crickets that threatened to decimate one of the first harvests in the Salt Lake Valley, which explicitly relate to present-day religious preoccupations. The 'lesson' from this lesson is easy – the timeless power of prayer brought a flock of seagulls to eat up the crickets.

Personal diaries, then, reproduce a version of history in which historical truth is subsumed under religious truth. Jon Mitchell (1998) has explored the relationship between religious and historical truth. He relates how for the Maltese, questions about whether the shipwreck of St Paul related by Luke in The Acts occurred on Malta or not are quickly resolved by reference to the 'truth' of the Bible. Yet, Mitchell also shows how these different kinds of 'truths' – historical and religious – become intertwined, particularly in Malta, where many historians are also priests, who, like Mormons, see history as a method of laying bare the ultimate religious truth. This relationship between religious and historical truth is not, however, always a harmonious one, and nor is it confined to Mormon diaries. The eminent Mormon historian Leonard Arrington has outlined several stages in Mormon Church history (Arrington 1992), each of which reflect a different relationship between these two versions of truth. The Church has always designated officials to record its history, and has kept records of meetings and other documents. The second stage of official Church history, according to Arrington, began with the preparation by Joseph Smith and his associates of a documentary record entitled the *History of Joseph Smith*. This type of documentary work was succeeded by the preparation of biographies of other Church leaders, and then by synthesis histories, and by the publication of various missionary tracts with historical sections. These include the many-times reissued *Essentials of Church History*, by Joseph Fielding Smith (1922) which was originally written as a manual for priesthood[5] classes. Some of the documentary histories of the Church were, according to Arrington, written to prove a theological thesis, 'such as that the Lord looked after the Saints' (Arrington 1992: 3). 'Above all,' though, says Arrington, 'our historians were perhaps unduly respectful of certain authorities, placing credence in accounts that should have been subjected to critical analysis' (ibid.). It is these studies which, Arrington argues, have set the tone for Mormon history – at least until the emergence of 'The New Mormon History' post 1950. This kind of history still finds a place in Church lesson manuals and in Church literature around historical sites, and is reproduced in diaries and personal journals.[6]

The reproductions contained in Mormon journals, and those which appear in other kinds of narrative or representations of historical sites and journeys, are at one level a continuation of a long tradition of Mormon history, in which theological truth and historical truth become combined. However, they also feed into a whole set of complex and mutually constitutive images and narrative forms.

The Mormon narrative form *par excellence* is the testimony. Testimonies are usually[7] 'borne' as part of a Sunday meeting called the Fast and Testimony meeting, which takes place on the first Sunday of every month. The main part of the meeting is given over to members of the congregation rather than to an address by assigned speakers or religious leaders. Members of the congregation usually go up to the stand (pulpit) and speak into the microphone. They will be doing what is called 'bearing their testimony'. Testimony meetings are held, according to a local Church leader, 'to strengthen each other by bearing testimony of the truthfulness of the gospel'. Testimonies therefore consist primarily of public expressions of personal religious conviction. However, they may also include narratives of spiritual experiences, expressions of thankfulness and appreciation to God and to members of the congregation, reflections on recent spiritual life events, such as attending the temple or completing the Seminary or Institute programmes, and sometimes public confessions, although the confessional form has declined since Church policy ceased to require public confession of sin as part of the repentance procedure. There is no strict form for a testimony and they are not prepared beforehand.[8] They are, ideally, spontaneous and reflect the fact that the speaker 'feels the spirit' and is prompted to bear his or her testimony.

However, lack of official and prepared structure does not mean that Mormon testimonies are unstructured and each one idiosyncratic. In fact, they follow a formula which allows for little deviation, the learning of which is an important part of learning to be a Mormon. As with other bodily practices, speech patterns and formulae are acquired, practised and embodied in the process of becoming, constituting and reconstituting the Mormon person (see Mitchell 2000). Both Armand Mauss (1994: 28–29) and David Knowlton (1991) have pointed to the importance of the 'ritual' of testimony bearing.

Recent anthropological use of linguistic theories, such as those of Austin (1962), has suggested that language should be explored in a way which is not restricted to its referential properties. This has informed work on conversion narratives (see e.g. Caldwell 1983; Harding 1987; Stromberg 1993), of which the testimony is one form. Importantly, Stromberg's work suggests that we must examine testimonies (and the events of their telling) for what they accomplish – they are not simply records of conversion events, they are constitutive acts which are a key part of the conversion process itself (Stromberg 1993).

Broadly speaking, there are three things that the conversion narrative or testimony can do. Firstly, through autobiography, it establishes a break with the narrator's past life, showing a resolution of spiritual conflict (see, e.g. Harrison 1989: 13). Stromberg argues that this resolution is accomplished partly through the learning of a new canonical language with which the conversion narrative itself is then constructed, and that this 'change in the believer's life is sustained only to the extent that it is continually constituted' through the retelling of the story (Stromberg 1993.) This links to the second act the testimony accomplishes – it requires the convert to learn a new 'language' (in the broadest, embodied sense). Thirdly, as the narration of the convert's own life is reconstituted in the canonical language and embodied being of the religion, the testimony allows the incorporation of personal experiences with cultural values (Knowlton 1991).

In the Mormon testimony these can be seen most clearly in a classic pattern which makes heavy use of Mormon history. A common theme in Mormon testimonies is the assertion of belief in the story of Joseph Smith's First Vision,[9] which forms Mormonism's origin myth (cf. Eliade 1964; Shipps 1987: 31–32). The reiteration of the story of the first vision, and, more importantly, assertions that it is true, in testimony after testimony, throughout the Mormon world, constantly reinforce this connection. Davies argues that the practice of referring to this story in bearing testimony shows a commitment to a particular theory of history (Davies 1989: 170), a theory of history in which God is a central character and force, as all history becomes the history of the Church itself (ibid.). However, the use of this story in the testimony also allows individual Mormons to enter into the myth themselves. As Knowlton says, it 'links the formative myth of Mormonism and the Saints' daily lives' (Knowlton 1991: 21). The 'First Vision' story is a symbol which is 'sufficiently multivalent to serve, on the one hand, as a "shared community experience ... that every Mormon must respond to personally", and, on the other, as a disseminator of agreement about things historical and a preserver of unity about matters doctrinal' (Shipps 1987: 32, citation from Allen 1980: 61). Mormons who bear testimony that they know that Joseph Smith was a prophet of God effectively link themselves with this myth and with the world-view which it accompanies.

The testimony borne at a Fast and Testimony meeting by Elder Smith, a young missionary in Manchester, is typical in this respect:

> Brothers and sisters, I am so grateful to be here on my mission. ... It is my desire that everyone in the Church can know the joy that comes through bringing the gospel to someone. ... I know this Church is true. I know that it is the only true Church on earth and that it was restored

by Joseph Smith, who was a prophet of God. I know that, through prayer, everyone can receive a witness that the Church is true. You may not have a vision, or angels, or anything like that, but you will know. I'm grateful for the opportunity to be here in Manchester, and I say these things in the name of Jesus Christ. Amen.

Through the use of the form of the original Mormon origin myth, or by direct reference to it as here, Mormons incorporate themselves into a community for whom this myth is formative.

The testimony itself then, illustrates the interconnectedness of history and theology for Mormons which is also apparent in the popular and official Mormon orientations to history (see above). Examination of personal journals written about Mormon historical sites reveals not only an interest in a particular version of history (reconstructed, spiritually educational, faith-promoting), but also a reproduction of the testimony form. Mac writes, on his visit to Nauvoo:

> What a wonderful place to serve a mission! What a wonderful place. It is hard to visualise the hardships the early members went through to establish this city, but it is a tribute to the man Joseph Smith and his leadership that so many people came and worked here. ... I would like to think that if I had been alive then, and heard the message, I would have come here.

The relationship of text to place, however, and the relationship of different kinds of narrative (both textual and nontextual), is a complex and mutually constitutive one. This fugue is played out in another of Mac's journal entries, written at the place about which he is writing, and referring to scripture in which that place itself appears.

> I am sitting almost in the shadow of Carthage Jail, within view of the window from which the dear Prophet Joseph Smith fell, being murdered in cold blood. We have just read D&C 135 and Hebrews 9: 16–18.

Here, persons, places and texts act upon each other to confirm Mac's testimony of the truthfulness of the Mormon Church. This perhaps is what lies at the heart of Mormon pilgrimage.

Photographs and postcards

However, it is not just texts such as *Joseph Smith – History* or the *Doctrine and Covenants* that are incorporated into the experience of place – and then reinscribed into journals and testimonies (which may then 'travel' with their narrators back home to yet another place). Other texts find their way into the experience of place. These are, in particular, scriptural texts which become monuments, and Church texts of various kinds which are produced on postcards and leaflets. My discussion of these texts necessarily introduces a new element into the person/place/text arrangement – that of image.

Amongst the personal journals, letters and postcards that I was lent for this research, I found a large number of photographs – not surprising, given the fact that photographs play a large role in modern touristic travel, and the fact that these Mormon pilgrimages are often simultaneously secular travel (some of the diaries contain detailed descriptions of which members of their party went on which Disney Land rides, or menu descriptions – 'I had cream of broccoli soup and crackers, then a roll and chicken breast in sauce, lettuce and green beans, followed by a chocolate "rock" (marshmallow) pie'). But I was struck by the number of photographs which depicted monuments, rather than sites, and, further, by the number of these monuments which were engravings of scriptural texts, or plaques (see Figures 1 and 2). On my own visits to sites in Utah I had been dimly aware of this use of text as monument, but the number of photos which showed these made a big impact.

This suggests a strong link between person, place and text – which is augmented by connections to images and objects. Also the importance of reproduction and reality – several photos show rooms as they would have been during the time of the incident which the plaque refers to, and some show 'the place', such as the 'sacred grove', where the First Vision is supposed to have taken place (although the exact location of the vision is unknown). This adds experience into the person/place/text equation. The use of evocation through reconstructed historical sites, as well as through strategies such as hymn singing, and the reading of scriptures in key places, suggests that individuals' experiences in particular places are made sacred through the ways in which persons, places and texts are

Figure 1 Scripture at Hill Cumorah Visitors' Centre. Photo: Jean Fields

Figure 2 Plaque marking 'The Sacred Grove'. Photo: Jean Fields

made to resonate in those places. The more that a particular place can be connected with either religious narratives or previous religious experiences (see Mitchell 2001), the more it is experienced as sacred. Photos here, as with souvenir photos more generally, show that this person was there –providing links in this case not only to the place, but also to the incidents which took place there.[10] This echoes the way in which the Mormon testimony allows personal experience to be constituted in canonical terms, demonstrating (a) commitment to Mormonism by going, (b) that you were there in that place by taking a photo, and (c) recognition that this place is important by taking photos which show plaques and official markers of importance and sacredness.

As I suggested in the introduction, attention needs to be paid to the structural and organisational aspects of pilgrimage. In this case, we can see Church control over texts which are linked to particular places, and thus Church attempts to influence the particular reading of a place. An LDS-produced leaflet available in Nauvoo, for example, contains a substantial section on 'The Church Today', and begins its historical exposition:

The story of Nauvoo and Carthage can't be told without briefly explaining why thousands of people would leave friends and families and the comfort of their homes to settle in a seemingly inhospitable spot. The story begins with the religious experiences of Joseph Smith.

Figure 3 Couple in the pose of Joseph and Emma Smith. Photo: Hannah Mitchell

The Church also influences the images associated with these places. Tourist leaflets such as the one cited above also contain images such as, for example, *The First Vision*, a painting by Greg K. Olsen. This picture will be familiar to all Mormons, as it is used extensively in Church literature. The Nauvoo experience is thus given the stamp of Church approval. This stamp of approval is also seen in a 'branding' of all kinds of literature with the name of the Church or the LDS Church logo (see Figure 4), a branding which extends to persons in the form of the badge worn by all missionaries, and to places in the form of plaques (see Figure 5).

Church control may also extend into the realm of the person of the visitor. In the case of the 'Sacred Grove', this extends to influencing the bodily deportment of visitors – as we might expect (cf. Mitchell 2000). A plaque at the 'Sacred Grove' states:

GOD TOLD THE PROPHET MOSES ON MOUNT HOREB, '… THE PLACE WHEREON THOU STANDEST IS HOLY GROUND' (EXODUS 3:5). BECAUSE GOD THE FATHER AND HIS SON JESUS CHRIST APPEARED TO JOSEPH SMITH IN THE SACRED GROVE, WE FEEL THAT THIS TOO IS HOLY GROUND. PLEASE SHOW REVERENCE WHILE VISITING THE GROVE. SPEAK IN SUBDUED TONES AND

The Church of Jesus Christ of Latter-day Saints
HILL CUMORAH
VISITORS' CENTER

Figure 4 LDS Church 'branding'

Figure 5 'Branding' plaque. Photo: Jean Fields.

ENJOY THE QUIET SPIRIT WHICH EXISTS HERE. TAKE THE TIME
TO MEDITATE AND CONSIDER THE VISION THE PROPHET JOSEPH
SMITH EXPERIENCED HERE IN THE SPRING OF 1820.

The portions of scripture which are reproduced in monuments are
often those which attest to the truthfulness of the Book of Mormon – thus
making the photos taken of them part of the testimony they bear. This is
furthered by the showing of these photos – Jean bears her testimony and
writes to me: 'I have sent these photos, hoping that they will be of use to
you ... Please return these photos as [they] may be of use to someone else.'

Non-Mormon writing

Elsewhere (Coleman 2001), I have been criticised for presenting Mormon
sacred travel as if it were homogenous. I am sensitive to this criticism,
although, as I argued above, I think that an overemphasis on
heterogeneity, creativity and the role of the individual pilgrim, while
representing an important development in pilgrimage and ritual studies,
is not necessarily helpful to an understanding of the Mormon case. Of

course there *are* differences in the ways that different Mormons experience their travels through their history, and I discuss some of these in detail below, but it is important to understand the extent to which the Mormon experience of history is successfully homogenised. The control of the substance of Church history is highly successful, in part through the merging of theology with history, as discussed above. Further, historiography has been the subject of a number of controversies within the Church during the past twenty years, and a number of prominent scholars have left or been forced out of their academic posts as a result (see e.g. Quinn 1992a, Knowlton 1994). Controversy *does* exist around issues of history; nevertheless, Mormon pilgrimage to historical sites often retains aspects of form and content, even when the individual is not a mainstream Mormon. Such a finding indicates the power of the embodied pilgrimage experience – embedded as it is in everyday Mormon life (see Mitchell 2001), and sacralised by the repetition and replication of key narratives. Below, I discuss an unpublished, but fairly widely circulated, essay written by an ex-Mormon.

'Ambivalence in Every Footstep' is a reflexive essay written by Troy Williams, who, after growing up as a Mormon in the U.S.A., and serving in the Bristol Mission in England, decided to identify himself firstly as a 'non-denominational' Mormon (a reference to the other schisms of Mormonism such as the RLDS Church and numerous polygamous groups, as well as the LDS Church), and then as a non-Mormon. In this essay, he writes about his experiences visiting historical sites on the Mormon history trail. In 1997, the Church celebrated the 150th anniversary of the arrival in the Salt Lake Valley with a programme of events under the banner 'Faith in Every Footstep'. Troy, as he says in the essay, decided to 'beat the rush and go a year early' on his personal quest for meaning in Mormon history. In the process he found not a testimony-building experience but great ambivalence, as he uncovered the dissonance between official or popular Mormon history, and that recounted in the non-Mormon history books he read.

In Troy's essay, we see again the importance of narrative, and we see again how the reproduction of canonical narrative form is made to serve a purpose. However, whilst in the cases discussed earlier the function of the narrative was to render particular sites and experiences sacred, here it serves a different purpose. Here, Troy reproduces familiar narrative, but subverts it. In particular, he is using irony (cf. Coleman and Elsner 1998) and playing with the testimony genre. Troy's demonstrated familiarity with the genre serves to justify his 'Mormon' credentials, but it is more than that. The experience that has become embodied during his early Mormon life does actually shape this confrontation with his past – even though he eventually breaks out of a simple replicating pattern. Although he states 'the Mormon Trail was a *sine qua non* destination on my spiritual itinerary. I had to go. I went searching for answers, I went searching for faith, but most of all, I went searching for identity', the identity he ends up with is not the Mormon one which our other pilgrims, Mac and Kathy, found, but one which steps outside the Mormon mainstream.

So, what aspects of narrative sacralisation are apparent in this essay, where do these diverge from the homogenised experience, and how is this possible in a Church which, as I have suggested above, exerts so much successful control over its history? Troy's narrative starts with a search for theological and historical truth, a goal which, as we saw above, is nurtured by the Mormon amalgamation of history and theology.

> I devoted myself to the historical and theological study of Mormonism. I believed quite honestly ... that studying the Mormon past would strengthen my testimony of the restored Gospel and Church to which I was born ... My expectations were met and exceeded in unexpected and challenging ways ... The study of my ancestors has become a spiritual journey into the wilderness of faith.

But here Troy introduces echoes of another narrative – *The Wilderness of Faith* is the title of an edited collection of essays by Mormon scholars and intellectuals, reflecting on crises in their personal testimonies of the Church (Stilitoe 1991). By introducing this narrative, Troy links his story with theirs, providing a new community or canonical language with which to tell his story. He also suggests links to other narratives, whose influences are missing from the standard Mormon version. His account of Nauvoo, for example, reads very differently to Kathy's:

> The Nauvoo LDS visitor center is what I would expect from an LDS visitor center. The various presentations focus on skeletal history, the

mission of Christ, and of course, 'families are forever'.[11] The Church video re-enactment of Nauvoo is the typical gloss and sentimentality that has become the standard from LDS films. Nauvoo residents circa 1844 are portrayed as happy, law-abiding, mainstream Christians, who simply cannot understand why mobs are hounding them. All presentations view the Saints as innocent victims and the mobs as vicious, evil predators. For balance and perspective I began reading several history books that focused on the Nauvoo era of the LDS epic. The story of Nauvoo Mormonism became far more disturbing than faithpromoting.

This introduction of the scholarly historical narrative – the history books he turns to in order to flesh out the story – is one of the main reasons that these sites are not successfully experienced by him as sacred.

What we can see here is the failure of narrative to sacralise Mormon history sites. There are two main reasons for this. Firstly, a noncanonical narrative is inserted into the person/place/text triad. In this case it is that of the academic historian. Secondly, and perhaps partly as a result of this, the individual's relationship to the testimony narrative is transformed. The feelings that are interpreted by others as indicating the presence of the spirit become separated from the circumstances of their inception, and, instead of being experienced as 'pure' spirit, are intellectualised and understood as 'emotional' (cf. Mitchell 1997). Such a rupture creates a disjunction between the individual and the community, a reversal, if you like, of Stromberg's process of conversion. In his heart, Troy must recognise this when he writes, 'Must the price of community be my individual soul?'.

Conclusion

I have argued that understanding religious travel requires an appreciation, not only of the ways in which individual pilgrims structure their own experiences, but of the ways in which institutional, organisational and authoritative structures impact upon places, persons and texts, making them more or less sacred. I have tried to show that this does not necessarily require a focus on homogeneity; indeed, I have argued that the interplay of person and place, facilitated by different kinds of texts, is the source both of homogeneity and heterogeneity. It is narrative, in its various forms, that is instrumental in constructing Mormon visits to historical sites as sacred, rather than secular, travel. Further, these narratives must be located in the wider Mormon experience, where 'the word' has a particular power through the testimony genre, and where authority lies in scripture. I have argued elsewhere that experiences in sacred sites must be understood in their relation to Mormon experiences in the temple and in everyday Mormon life. The interplay between person, place and text discussed here follows a similar pattern.

It would be foolish, however, to assume that Mormon travel around historical sites can be exclusively categorised as 'pilgrimage'. As I noted at the start of this paper, Mormon 'pilgrimage' does not entail either a penitential or a miraculous aspect. Such a finding suggests that this kind of travel may have more in common with secular travel or tourism than traditional pilgrimage. Locating the analysis within the triad of person/place/text, however, serves to highlight both the ways in which it does make sense to talk of Mormon 'pilgrimage' and the ways in which Mormon travel is simultaneously secular. I have suggested that sites are made sacred by a particular conjunction of person, place and text, and that the same sites will not be experienced as sacred where this does not happen. Other sites or activities which form part of the same visit or holiday (e.g. visiting relatives or theme parks, eating out, theatre trips and so on) are not subject to this interplay of person/place/text, and are thus experienced purely as holiday activities.

Coleman and Elsner, in the move away from a structural approach to pilgrimage, have tried to focus our attention on to the ways in which individual creativity and irony come into play in the active construction of the pilgrimage experience. I have argued here that, in the case of religions such as Mormonism, closer attention than usual has to be paid to the ways in which individuals are affected by the nature of their church organisations. Attention to the ways in which people construct their own spirituality is valuable, but often neglects the constraints which religious frameworks can impose (see Asad 1983). In looking at how the person/place/text triad plays out in Mormon pilgrimage, however, we have seen how these two things are more integrated than might be supposed. Kathy, Mac and Troy each author their own accounts of their encounters with the Mormon past, making use, in various ways, of the forms, themes, images and motifs which surround them, in both their religious and secular lives.

Notes

1 These are study programmes run by the Church for secondary school-aged children and university-aged students respectively.
2 The problem of how to reconcile Church interpretations of historical events with those of academic historians has received attention in recent writings by Mormon scholars and historians. Prolific Mormon historian D. Michael Quinn has written about how he believes he was excommunicated by the Church for his academic work (Quinn 1992a), and has edited a volume in which a number of scholars reflect on their problematic relationship with the Church and their Discipline (Quinn 1992b).
3 'Mormons' are members of The Church of Jesus Christ of Latter-day Saints. 'Mormon' was originally a derogatory term, derived from the church's book of scripture, the Book of Mormon.
4 Members of the Church refer to themselves as 'saints', from the full name of the Church – The Church of Jesus Christ of Latter-day Saints.
5 The Mormon priesthood is not a restricted order, and there is no particular special training prior to ordination to its various ranks. All men deemed worthy by their leaders can hold the priesthood. Priesthood holders are instructed together on Sundays, while the women are instructed in their 'Relief Society' meetings.
6 Importantly, this kind of history has been challenged by those who form part of 'The New Mormon History'. See, for example, the book of that name, edited by D. Michael Quinn (1992b), as well as Quinn's article, 'On Being a Mormon Historian (and its Aftermath)', in which he candidly discusses the intellectual and spiritual perils facing religious historians of history (Quinn 1992a).
7 Testimonies are not exclusive to the Fast and Testimony meeting – they may also be borne at other occasions, 'when the spirit moves' people to do so, and they may also be written down.
8 Mormon prayers, with the exception of the Sacrament prayer and prayers for saving ordinances of baptism, confirmation etc., are not preprepared. Temple dedicatory prayers and patriarchal blessings are written down afterwards, since they are considered to be divine revelation.
9 The canonical and indeed scriptural account of 'First Vision' can be read in *Joseph Smith – History* in *The Pearl of Great Price*, which is published with the *Doctrine and Covenants*.
10 A variation on this theme can also be seen in photos which reproduce images from popular pictures of from monuments, such as statues dedicated to marriage or to women (see Figure 3).
11 'Families are forever' is a motto of the Church and refers to its belief in the doctrine of 'eternal' or 'celestial marriage', which is not 'till death do us part'.

References

Allen, J. (1980) 'Emergence of a Fundamental: The Expanding Role of Joseph Smith's First Vision in Mormon Religious Thought', *Journal of Mormon History*, 7: 43–61.

Arrington, L. (1992) 'The Search for Truth and Meaning in Mormon History', in D. Michael Quinn (ed.) *The New Mormon History: Revisionist Essays on the Past*. Salt Lake City: Signature Books, pp. 1–12.

Asad, T., (1983) 'Anthropological Conceptions of Religion: Reflections on Geertz', *Man*, 18(2): 237–59.

Austin, J. (1962) *How to Do Things with Words*. Oxford: Clarendon Press.

Bourdieu, P. (1990) *The Logic of Practice*. Cambridge: Polity Press.

Bowman, G. (2000) 'Christian Ideology and the Image of the Holy Land: The Place of Jerusalem Pilgrimage in the Various Christianities', in J. Eade and M. Sallnow (eds) *Contesting the Sacred: The Anthropology of Christian Pilgrimage*. Urbana and Chicago: University of Illinois Press (First Edition, 1991, London: Routledge).

Buerger, D. (1994) *The Mysteries of Godliness: A History of Mormon Temple Worship*. San Francisco, C.A.: Smith Research Associates.

Caldwell, P. (1983) *The Puritan Conversion Narrative: The Beginnings of American Expression*. Cambridge: Cambridge University Press.

The Church of Jesus Christ of Latter-day Saints (1995) [1979]. *Truth Restored: A Short History of the Church of Jesus Christ of Latter-day Saints*. Church of Jesus Christ of Latter-day Saints, Salt Lake City, Utah.

—— (1985) [1830]. *The Book of Mormon*. Copyright 1981 by the Corporation of the President of The Church of Jesus Christ of Latter-day Saints, Salt Lake City, Utah.

—— (1985) *Doctrine and Covenants*. Copyright 1981 by the Corporation of the President of The Church of Jesus Christ of Latter-day Saints, Salt Lake City, Utah.

—— (1985) *The Pearl of Great Price*. Copyright 1981 by the Corporation of the President of The Church of Jesus Christ of Latter-day Saints, Salt Lake City, Utah.

—— (1992) *Follow Me: Relief Society Personal Study Guide 4*. Corporation of the President of The Church of Jesus Christ of Latter-day Saints, Salt Lake City, Utah.

Coleman, S. (2000) *The Globalisation of Charismatic Christianity: Spreading the Gospel of Prosperity*. Cambridge University Press: Cambridge.

—— (2001) 'Bringing Structure Back In', *Anthropology Today*. Vol 17, No 3, June.

Coleman, S. and Elsner, J. (1995) *Pilgrimage: Sacred Travel and Sacred Space in the World Religions*. Cambridge, M.A.: Harvard University Press.

————— (1998) 'Performing Pilgrimage: Walsingham and the Ritual Construction of Irony', in F. Hughes-Freeland (ed.) *Ritual, Performance, Media*. London: Routledge, pp. 46–65.

Davies, D. (1989) 'On Mormon History, Identity and Faith Community', in E. Tonkin, M. McDonald and M. Chapman (eds) *History and Ethnicity*. Association of Social Anthropologists of the Commonwealth Monographs: Volume 27 London: Routledge.

—— (2000) *The Mormon Culture of Salvation*. Aldershot: Ashgate Press.

Eade, J. and Sallnow, M. (eds) (2000) *Contesting the Sacred: The Anthropology of Christian Pilgrimage*. Urbana and Chicago: University of Illinois Press (First Edition 1991, London: Routledge).

Eliade, M., (1963) 'Sacred places: temple, palace, "centre of the world", in *Patterns in Comparative Religion*, New York: World Publishing Co.

—— (1964) *Myth and Reality*. New York: Harper and Row.

Gold, A. (1988) *Fruitful Journeys: The Ways of Rajasthani Pilgrims*. Berkeley, C.A.: University of California Press.

Harding, S. (1987) 'Convicted by the Holy Spirit: The Rhetoric of Fundamental Baptist Conversion', *American Ethnologist*, 14(1): 167–81.

Harrison, J. (1989) 'The Popular History of Early Victorian Britain: A Mormon Contribution', in R. Jensen and M. Thorpe (eds) *Mormons in Early Victorian Britain*. Salt Lake City: University of Utah Press, pp.1–15.

Karve, I. (1962) 'On the Road: A Maharashtrian Pilgrimage', *Journal of Asian Studies*, 22: 13–30.

Knowlton, D. (1991) 'Belief, Metaphor and Rhetoric: The Mormon Practice of Testimony Bearing', *Sunstone*, April 1991.

—— (1994) 'The Unspeakable and Intellectual Politics in Mormonism'. Unpublished paper. [An earlier version of this paper was given at the 1992 *Sunstone* Symposium, Salt Lake City, Utah, under the title 'Secrecy, Deceit and the Sacred in Mormonism'.]

Mauss, A. (1994) *The Angel and the Beehive: The Mormon Struggle With Assimilation*. Urbana and Chicago: University of Illinois Press.

Mitchell, H. (2000) 'Belief, Activity and Embodiment in the Constitution of Contemporary Mormonism'. PhD thesis, Queens University of Belfast.

—— (2001) '"Being There": British Mormons and the History Trail', *Anthropology Today*, 17(2) (April): 9–14.

Mitchell, J. (1997) 'A Moment with Christ: The Importance of Feelings in the Analysis of Belief', *Journal of the Royal Anthropological Institute*. 3(1): 79–94.

—— (1998) 'A Providential Storm: Myth, History and the Story of St Paul's Shipwreck in Malta', in *Memory, History and Critique: European Identity at the Millennium*. Proceedings of the Fifth Conference of the International Society for the Study of European Ideas (ISSEI).

Quinn, D. (1992a) 'On Being a Mormon Historian (and its Aftermath)', in G. Smith (ed.) *Faithful History: Essays on Writing Mormon History*. Salt Lake City, Signature Books.

—— (1992b) (ed.) *The New Mormon History: Revisionist Essays on the Past*. Salt Lake City: Signature Books.

Rabinow, P. (1975) *Symbolic Domination: Cultural Form and Historical Change in Morocco*. Chicago: University of Chicago Press.

Shipps, J. (1987) *Mormonism: The Story of a New Religious Tradition*. Urbana and Chicago: University of Illinois Press.

Smith, J. (1922) *Essentials of Church History*. Salt Lake City: Deseret Book Company.

Stilitoe, J. (ed.) (1991) *The Wilderness of Faith: Essays on Contemporary Mormon Thought*. Salt Lake City: Signature Books.

Stirrat, R. (2000) 'Place and Person in Sinhala Catholic Pilgrimage', in J. Eade, and M. Sallnow (eds), *Contesting the Sacred: The Anthropology of Christian Pilgrimage*. Urbana and Chicago: University of Illinois Press (first edition, 1991, London: Routledge).

Stromberg, P. (1993) *Language and Self-transformation: A Study of the Christian Conversion Narrative*. Cambridge: Cambridge University Press.

Troeltsch, E. (1931) *The Social Teaching of the Christian Churches*, trans. O. Wyon, London: Macmillan.

Turner, V. and Turner, E. (1978) *Image and Pilgrimage in Christian Culture: Anthropological Perspectives.* Oxford: Blackwell.

Williams, T. (ND) 'Ambivalence in Every Footstep: The Journey of a Non-Denominational Mormon', unpublished manuscript.

Woodward, K. (1996) *Making Saints: How the Catholic Church Determines Who Becomes a Saint, Who Doesn't, and Why*, 2nd edn. New York: Simon and Schuster.

Index

* Index compiled by Verity Platt